YEHUDI MENUHIN MUSIC GUIDES

Piano

YEHUDI MENUHIN MUSIC GUIDES

Available
Clarinet by Jack Brymer
Flute by James Galway
Violin and Viola by Yehudi Menuhin and William Primrose

YEHUDI MENUHIN MUSIC GUIDES

Piano

Louis Kentner

KAHN & AVERILL, LONDON

This edition first published in 1991 by
Kahn & Averill
9 Harrington Road, London SW7 3ES

First published in Great Britain in 1976 by
Macdonald and Jane's Publishers Ltd

British Library Cataloguing in Publication Data
Kentner, Louis 1905-1987
    Piano. – (Yehudi Menuhin music guides; v.3)
    1. Piano playing
    I Title   II. Series
    786.214

    ISBN 1-871082-18-8

Printed in Great Britain by
Halstan & Co Ltd., Amersham, Bucks

Contents

List of Illustrations

List of Illustrations

ACKNOWLEDGEMENTS

Editorial board:

General editor: Yehudi Menuhin

Coordinating editor: Patrick Jenkins

Advisers: Martin Cooper
Eric Fenby
Robert Layton
Denis Stevens

Drawings: Ian Fleming and Associates

Music examples: Malcolm Lipkin

The purpose of this series is not to impose a new set of musical disciplines, nor to attempt to provide a blue-print for yet another teaching 'method'; but to stimulate in the musical young (as well as students of all ages) a still finer, and better informed, response to the instruments of their choice and to the world of music they contain.   P. J.

Editor's Introduction
by Yehudi Menuhin

It gives me particular pleasure that the 'Music Guides' series should be inaugurated by this fascinating dissertation on the piano by Louis Kentner.

It is typical of this distinguished man and musician that he has given us neither an arid 'theory' nor an abstract 'method', but rather the feeling of sharing in a train of thought and music, thus bringing to the reader the concern of a great performer for the understanding of his audience. It is characteristic of Louis Kentner that every thought serves the interpretation, the meaning and message of music. Nor, where there is a technical analysis, is it ever a mere attitude, distant from the ultimate purpose, but arises organically from the very substance of which music is made: quality of sound, depth of meaning, range of colour. And above and through all in its integrity and honesty can be heard the voice of the supreme artist.

Together with Kentner's words, in fact, the perspicacious reader shares the man and the musician alike – his genius, his humour, his affection, his joie-de-vivre, his enormous musical maturity, his vast experience and his clarity. This is a rare privilege, and one which will be rewarding not only to any music-lover, be he amateur, professional or (like myself) one of the many who are well acquainted with the art of Louis Kentner, but also – such is the quality of this book in terms of human and civil value – to even the casual reader who is curious to understand the mysteries of music and the artist's mind, the sensitive heart and the disciplined hands that make music possible.

Yehudi Menuhin

1

A Letter, by Way of Introduction

To Patrick Jenkins, Esq.

My dear Patrick,

Like the prisoner about to be condemned to death I shall, in due course, claim the right to speak in my own defence before sentence is pronounced. Only, not having committed a crime more serious than that of writing a book, I propose to make use also of the additional prerogative of entering my plea – a plea of 'guilty' on some counts, of 'not guilty' on others – even before proceedings open. But, more than anything, I want the letter now before you to carry a message of affection and gratitude to you. Affection and gratitude because the two are inseparable, in my view: affection is in itself a boon to be grateful for (whether you are receiving or dispensing it), and gratitude cannot be felt without affection. To your sturdy encouragement I owe this book. The thanks of a newly-hatched writer – probably not much of a writer at that, but one whose twin inhibitions of natural diffidence and lack of experience your sure and benevolent judgement helped to remove – the thanks of this writer go to you for causing this book to be written. If there is any good in it the credit shall be yours – and so will be the execration if the book turns out to be rotten.

I suppose almost every author has the wish to explain himself; and I can see you patiently preparing to undergo the inevitable, whereas anyone else would cut the ordeal short by urging, 'Get on with it and let the book speak for itself.' The fact is, there always remains something to be explained, something personal, something that cannot be accommodated in the text or in footnotes. For example, it is obvious that in a book of this kind lucidity takes precedence over thorough comprehensiveness. I did not try to answer all the questions but rather to make such answers as are to be found clear and unequivocal. Limiting the ground to be covered thus became imperative.

I anticipate criticism, especially of Part III, of the following kind: 'Why no analysis of such meritorious piano music as Haydn's or Mozart's sonatas? Why is Weber only mentioned *en passant*? Why almost nothing about Schumann? About Brahms?' Some will demand justice for Prokofiev, or want more space for Bartók – all valid objections, without any doubt. If this book had been planned as a compendium of piano literature my selection would have been a much more catholic one. But I had to remind myself from time to time that the theme was – the piano.

Even so, certain omissions are in need of defence. Of course Weber was a highly significant composer, and his piano output, which includes four sonatas, cannot be ignored by specialists of the post-Mendelssohn pre-Chopin era. These works, however, are not often heard nowadays and – dare I say it? – there seems to be hanging about them a slightly musty smell of decay, the fading charm of 'period' art. At any rate, Weber's principal sphere of influence was the opera, his best medium the orchestra, not the piano – which appears happily married to the orchestra only once in Weber's work: in the still popular 'Conzertstück' in F minor. The 'period' label, with all its laudatory, and pejorative, connotations, fits also Mendelssohn's piano music. There is plenty of charm in some of the Songs Without Words, but somehow we seem to have outgrown them since Queen Victoria's time. Like Weber's best work, Mendelssohn's was done in orchestral and choral music, where his technical mastery secures him a place among the distinguished. Had he only composed his piano works, I fear Mendelssohn would be forgotten today.

And what about Schumann, perhaps the hardest sacrifice of all? There is hardly a musician who has not had, at some period of his early life, a passionate infatuation with Schumann's music – and there is hardly one who succeeded in prolonging this love affair into later life. Perhaps because Schumann was a young man's composer *par excellence*, an embodiment of romantic art, of romantic emotion – or perhaps because of certain technical faults which a more mature critical judgement could not fail to uncover – for whatever reason, the Schumann fever of the young is quickly burnt out. But it is ecstatic while it lasts. It is true that certain works, albeit no longer as popular as they were some 50 years ago, still appear from time to time in our concert halls, performed more often (be it noted) by young artists! I hope readers will forgive me if I – no longer a very young man – allow myself to be swayed to this extent by personal inclination: in regretfully leaving Schumann's pianistic contribution undiscussed (undeniably important though it was at its time), I follow the rule to keep silent when unable to praise.

Also I confess to a blind spot (but one with a different syndrome) in the case of Brahms. There can be no doubt: Brahms was a master composer, a strong personality, a follower of high ideals. But – all my life I have been beset by a lack of affinity, or what is now fashionable to call 'empathy', with this master's piano music. In particular (with the exceptions of the two great concerti and the Paganini Variations – works I still perform quite frequently) it seemed to me to be lacking in colour and vividness, in beauty of sound – no matter how well it is played – and perhaps a little too full of *petit-bourgeois* sentiment inherited from Schumann and Mendelssohn. If Weber gave his best in opera, Schumann in lieder, Mendelssohn in choral music, then Brahms is surely at his best in chamber music (unless you are an out-an-out *aficionado* and believe him to be another Beethoven-size symphonist), certainly not in piano music.

This applies – *mutatis mutandis* – to the Haydn and the Mozart piano sonatas. Haydn's greatness lies enshrined in the string quartets – sublime masterpieces every one of them – and Mozart was supreme master of the piano concerto (an art form he virtually invented), and of course, by common consent, of opera. Neither of these masters should be

5

designated as a piano composer. Mozart's concerti, however, will be discussed in the chapter 'The piano combined with other instruments'.

These approximately are the reasons why some great and some distinguished composers were left out of my gallery of piano composers, that is to say, of composers who have given their best to the piano and to whom the piano has, in turn, revealed its mysteries. Beethoven was, of course, great in all fields, he could not be omitted. And in my last chapter, dealing with the post-Lisztian era, I did not disregard the so-called impressionists – Debussy and Ravel – not because of any over-riding claims they may have as piano composers but because of the influence they have exercised on our age and our piano-playing habits.

Perhaps I should say a word about why Prokofiev and Bartók are merely mentioned in Part III, without any attempt at detailed analysis. The reason is simple: anything that is still under controversy and dispute amongst musicians has to be automatically excluded from a book which does not propose to enter into controversy of any kind but presents objective fact, coloured, perhaps, by subjective viewings. Prokofiev and Bartók, both striking exceptions to the rule 'Nemo propheta in patria sua', are accepted as master composers in their respective countries, but in many other parts of the world they are still 'sub judice'. In this – and only in this – their cases are similar.

I hope to satisfy you in the matter of piano teaching, history and technique, although these subjects can occupy only one chapter each in a book of this size.

Other writers on my subject will be mentioned in due course, and sometimes quoted. But most of my views come from practical experience in playing, and teaching, the piano, supplemented by listening to the playing of others. In this context it was obviously necessary to mention some of the fine pianists of the past – with here and there a vignette about their playing – but I could not venture into our modern times by critically evaluating any outstanding young artists now before the public.

All musical examples are quoted from memory (without reference to the scores) and in a sort of musical shorthand; their aim is usually to illustrate some point, not to present the printed text accurately.

And if my final conclusions appear to be somewhat pessimistic – I refer to the short 'Epilogue' chapter – I can assure you that nobody would be happier to be proved wrong than myself.

In this hope I recommend the book to your continued benevolence, and remain, yours ever affectionately,

Louis Kentner

One
Apology, by Way of Further Introduction

An apology is always a good way of beginning a book. For even when all the portents are in his favour – when brilliant talent for writing is allied to profound knowledge of a subject which just happens to be one of universal appeal – an author must by common consent secure for himself an amused tolerance, if not downright benevolence, on the part of the reader; and he can do this only by adopting a becoming diffidence of demeanour. How much more so when the dice are loaded against him? He is not a born writer and the subject of his book is a very specialized one, of interest only to a small fraction of the community. He has a reasonably detailed *practical* knowledge of the subject (this must be admitted in common fairness) but it is badly in need of arraying, of putting in order, of finding connections between things seemingly unconnected, by means of thought-processes not normally required from a mere practitioner of his instrument.

I fear, therefore, that my apology is in order. Even more so when we think of the instrument in question. Has it not been called every name by music-lovers and -haters alike? Has it not fallen into disrepute, as the untalented amateur's favourite form of self-expression? A percussion instrument masquerading as an orchestra? The conductor's chosen appliance of torture, his revenge on singers and other soloists invading the rehearsal room? The Vienna offices of a famous music publishers' firm boasted the worst upright piano (so it was said) in the world: its purpose was to discourage arrogant young composers who, on hearing the dreadful sound of their works emanating under their fingers from this instrument, immediately and spontaneously reduced any monetary demands they had intended to make on the publishers by about half; this piano was known in Vienna as the '*Entmutigungsklavier*' ('piano for discouraging').

But I do not intend recording only pejorative comments about the hero of this book, the pianoforte. There were other, human heroes – dreamers, visionaries like Chopin, Liszt, and Anton Rubinstein – who proclaimed that the piano could sing, weep, whisper and thunder; that it had a soul. The scientists deny this, and no doubt the scientists must be right. They also deny that there is such a thing as 'touch' (as applied to a single note), maintaining that the pianoforte is capable only of soft and loud – as its name implies – and that all else must therefore be classed as figments of the imagination. This assertion, plausible enough on the face of it, should be subjected to critical scrutiny, if only to plead that figments of the imagination, or figments of the consciousness, do exist, in the sense in which everything else in our world is deemed to exist. And so it is perhaps possible that the fantasists who thought the piano capable of producing sounds other than soft and loud were not so far wrong after all. Vindication of the Chopin–Liszt–Rubinstein kind of thinking does not automatically mean that the scientists are wrong, but merely that the truth has many facets.

Metaphysics, then, gets a chance of a quick bow on our limited stage. And, in a book about the piano, I cannot avoid speaking about the way, or ways, of playing the instrument, a subject I shall try to deal with as exhaustively as possible, at the proper time. Impartial judgement on such things as teaching methods, matters of a technical nature in what is sometimes called 'keyboard treatment', or any other controversial theme connected with our main subject, will not, I hope, be expected from me; for, by the very fact of being a professional executant musician, I am wedded to a way of thinking and of doing things which must be my own. To have convictions implies the belief that contrary convictions held by others must be erroneous. This is true only in the limited area where such notions as 'right' and 'wrong' can be allowed to exist. Piano technique is not only governed by physiological and anatomical laws (subject, therefore, to the rigid categories of right and wrong), but also by imponderables from the uncharted regions of psychology, and here those who seek after truth must tread cautiously.

Every teacher knows that it is possible to be musically gifted but motorically weak, inhibited in the matter of muscular reaction yet responsive to music as such – it would be a pity to condemn all such individuals as unfit to play the piano. Rather it is a problem to be dealt with lovingly by the pedagogues.

Far be it from me to deny the immense value of the artist's instinct. The greater the artist the less fallible will be his intuition, the less he will have to be instructed in the conscious use of his faculties, which serve him well and can be quite effortlessly invoked from his subconscious mind by mental or physical automatisms evolved in a lifetime of practice. Such an exceptionally gifted person can afford to ignore what a detailed analytical investigation into the nature of his instrument could reveal, because his intuition will invariably lead him to choose the best and simplest way of treating that instrument. But what of the less gifted, the rank and file, the music lovers who battle with the instrument because no one has explained to them the relation in which it stands to the human anatomy? And even artists! I doubt if it would really rob a great pianist of his natural bloom to learn something about his piano. Moreover I have often blushed with shame at the thought that pianists (myself included) are as a rule unable to tune the piano or to put on a new string, things that every violinist knows how to do. Later on I hope to outline the essential facts about what is meant by the expression 'well-tempered' in Bach's great work. It is not to be confused with 'good tempered'. (See Chapter 4.)

But ignorance is not to be defended on any grounds – not even on those of genius. It is, of course, perfectly possible for a performer of genius to live out the whole of his artistic life relying entirely on his infallible intuition, and for such an intuitive (and ignorant) artist to reach the highest pinnacles of fame and success. Nevertheless, given an equality of talent, the perfectionist who has not only instinct but also knowledge at his disposal is my choice of artist. So I have devoted the first part of this book to a study of the workings of the piano, and the art of piano-tuning.

On a different, but closely related, level, it is clear that our age exacts a deeper involvement from artists in techno-logical matters, such as of recording or broadcasting, that in the old days used to be left to the specialists. There is no doubt that the artist who is not too proud to study the nature of microphones (or even, in some cases, of computers!) will make better recordings than the one who is content to mind his own narrowly-understood business – and better recordings mean, from the recipient's point of view, better performances and, therefore, better performers. We may deplore this state of things but we cannot alter it. What could follow from this more logically than the inexorable need to study the laws governing the relationship between our instrument, the piano, and the machine that records its sound? So after a full discussion of playing technique I do deal briefly, in the chapter on mechanical reproduction, with the two questions: should the player change his style of playing for recording purposes, and should the instrument intended for such purposes receive some sort of special treatment by the makers?

It is not my aim to go very thoroughly into the historical background: how the piano came into being, how it evolved from early forms, through harpsichord, clavichord, via the old square piano, right down to the concert grand of the concert hall – to trace all this, accurately and in full detail, is not the object of this book, interesting though the task would be to an historian. I simply touch upon this part of our story in a single chapter (Chapter 5) – and I handle even more lightly the sociological aspect, the part the piano's evolution has played in the evolution of human society, a subject which deserves a book to itself if it is to be treated in suitable depth.

Enough apologies! Let us plunge in *medias res*.

Part One:

Understanding the Piano

Two
The Instrument

Nothing has ever brought home to me more forcibly the nature of the pianoforte than a scene from a Marx Brothers film seen many years ago. In this scene the dumb character Harpo sets about destroying a concert grand piano (I do not remember why) by furious hammer blows. When he has succeeded in reducing the lid, the body, the pedals and the keyboard to an unrecognizable mass of rubbish, only the inner cavity – sound-board, strings and iron frame – surviving, Harpo is seen to realize that this part of the piano looks exactly like a harp; happy in this discovery, he finds to his utmost delight that it not only looks like a harp but can be played like one, which he then proceeds to do, most beautifully.

Let us overlook the poetic licence in this. The pedals of the harp (the real harp) which offer the possibility of unlimited chromatic transposition, must have been flown miraculously to the scene and fixed up by some Arabian Nights genie – or did Harpo use the old-fashioned chromatic harp? Such pedantic doubts never came to disturb my mind: the effect was most revealing, and made it clear in a flash that the piano was the child of a marriage between harp and organ, and had inherited some of the best qualities of its parents.

There is no doubt: the piano can sound like a harp, or almost, and it can, almost, sound like an organ. To the sharply defined 'plucking' effects, already known to the old masters of the harpsichord (clearly recognizable as one of the piano's ancestors), the piano makers have added, in centuries of patient effort, the possibility of sustaining sound, not only by means of pedalling, but also manually, by improvements in the sound-board mechanism. This great achievement of manual legato, or near-legato, makes the piano of today a close relation of the organ. It also brings it nearer to that most perfect of all instruments, the orchestra, the sound of which surely every good pianist sets out to imitate. The organ, as we know, does this by mechanical means, by pulling out stops: we get deceptively lifelike imitations of the sound of the viola, the oboe, the human voice and so forth, in bewildering variety and perfection, varying only as the organ builder's power covers a smaller or greater range of registration; little is left to human flesh and blood and its contact with the inanimate instrument. The primeval relationship of player and instrument is reversed, the instrument plays the musician.

With our instrument, the piano, we cannot hope to produce such perfect imitations. The greatest pianist, however, can do something that is both more and less than the mechanical perfection achieved on the organ. He can merge his body with that of the instrument, his mind with that of the music, and produce that triple unity of music, player and instrument which to many musicians is the ideal of music making.

The organ, for all its majestic richness of sound, tends to be a little heartless and inflexible: the piano makes up for its insufficient sustaining power by greater mobility and livelier speech, the greater art of heart-to-heart communication. If the organ is a great cathedral for worshipping the deity, then the piano is the comfortable house for people to live in. But it can be more than that. No one wants to live in a cathedral; but there is no reason why a believer in God should not worship him within his own four walls.

The all-purpose nature of the instrument opened up the way for its spectacular invasion into drawing rooms all over the world, an invasion which lasted for over a century and which is only now being partially replaced by another invasion, that of radio and television, to which it is gradually giving way. To this subsidence of the once all-powerful pianoforte as an integral part of every self-respecting household one contributory factor was the emergence of the gramophone, deflecting as it did so many music lovers not only from the pleasures of the concert hall (especially scientists who take a

16

Plate 1. Upright piano by Friederici di Gera, 1745.
Conservatoire Royal de Musique, Brussels.

professional interest in the mysteries of the microphone), but also from the once highly popular pastime of making one's own music, however badly, in one's own home, with one's own hands. Here, however, it is easy to detect a fallacy: to make a piano record, you still need a piano, and a pianist. I can foresee the time when records (very good ones, too) will be made without anyone playing; but this time is not yet. The gramophone has not, so far, totally replaced live music; there are hopeful signs of a continuing interest in the piano among the younger generation.

Plate 2. Mahogany grand piano, with gilded ornaments and painted decorations and landscapes. Made for Mr F. W. Woolworth and delivered in 1902.

Plate 3. The first White House Steinway, built in 1903.

Three
The Structure of the Piano

Let us now take a glance at this curious organ with the harp-shaped heart, so inadequate and yet in many ways so satisfying, and let us define its true nature.

Practical minds amongst musicians tend to limit their interest in the mechanics of the pianoforte to a fair minimum of knowledge – just sufficient, in fact, to provide them with an adequate assessment, gained through practice and experience, of what will be the likely result, in terms of sound, of certain physical actions on the part of the player. What goes on inside the instrument, how results are reached, by what mechanical ingenuities 'dreamed up' by the makers, are we, the artists, enabled to live in our different dreams – the exploration of the why and wherefore is usually left to the mechanically- and the scientifically-minded.

No one will deny the great value of empiricism in art when allied to outstanding talent and the instinct (which it was once fashionable to call 'serendipity') of making discoveries by accident. But there is a certain fascination in knowledge for its own sake – especially when it gives a more solid and lasting foundation even to a successful empiricism. Careful study of these diagrams and the simple descriptions is recommended to those whose desire is for knowledge as well as experience.

No one can seriously maintain that the modern pianoforte is a thing of beauty, in terms of drawing-room elegance or furniture appeal. The graceful shape of the harp, hidden in the inner cavity of the instrument, is, of course, invisible to any outside eye; the rest presents just a vast, clumsy, highly polished expanse of unlovely surface. No wonder piano makers right down the ages have endeavoured to express artistry and imagination in the design of this dreary outer shell, part cradle, part cupboard. Some results of their efforts, as shown here, are indeed not wholly unsuccessful. Some play is also made with colours (as there is, in fact, no reason why a piano should always be black or dark brown), but unhappily it must be admitted that even at its best the pianoforte cannot compete in shape and colour with string or wind instruments.

Perhaps it was for this reason that the less bulky upright, which can be unobtrusively accommodated in a modest corner, gained ascendancy in Victorian drawing rooms over the 'grand', its inferiority of tone and action notwithstanding. The upright has a much smaller action than the grand, this action being built perpendicularly into an elevated case above the keyboard, and consequently it has a much smaller tonal range. Nevertheless Chopin, one of the greatest piano composers of all times, is reputed to have preferred hearing his compositions played on upright pianos: perhaps his morbidly sensitive, mimosa-like soul shrank from the noise with which he felt a grand piano would assail his ear – and no doubt some performers even today are guilty of producing an unnecessarily ugly sound when they wish to play forcefully. Liszt, too, can be seen on contemporary daguerreotypes, sitting, surrounded by his pupils, at an upright piano – which proves that the '*Jupiter tonans*' image of Liszt, producing thunder and lightning from a huge concert grand, must have been a falsification of the truth, and that the 'still small voice' (the Chopin voice) was not alien to him. Be that as it may, we know today that the big concert grand can not only roar and thunder; it can also whisper if necessary, given the proper treatment by the proper player.

But it must be said: except for practical reasons – such as saving space, or saving the grand the wear and tear of daily practice (some of which can be done quite reasonably on an upright), or being kind to the neighbours – the upright piano has no artistic justification whatsoever.

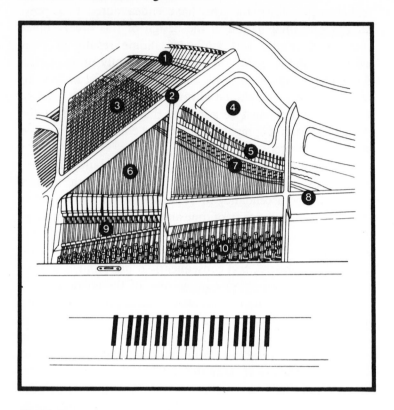

Grand piano

1 Bass bridge	7 Treble bridge
2 Plate	8 Bearing bar (integral with the
3 Bass strings	plate)
4 Sound-board	9 Agraffes
5 Hitch pins	10 Tuning pins
6 Dampers	

The action: key, hammer and strings

For those who feel that the mechanics of the piano action must be explained before I can show how the anatomy of the human body affects it, let me quote some relevant and succinct pages from Tobias Matthay's book *Pianoforte Tone Production* – a work as epoch-making for piano teaching at the time (1903) as, say, Freud's *Interpretation of Dreams* was for psychiatric practitioners – and as bitterly attacked by die-hards.*

At the pianoforte, the requisite concussions that form sound are communicated to the atmosphere by means of to-and-fro motions (vibrations) of the string, enhanced by the sounding-board. The greater the *number* of such vibrations completed by the string per second, the higher (more acute in pitch) is the resulting note. The

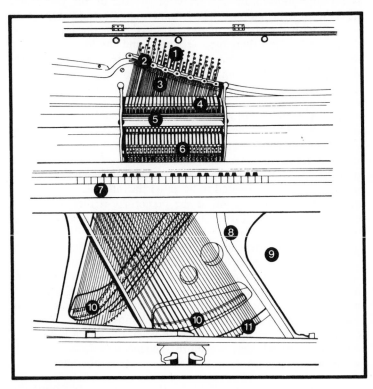

Upright piano

1 Tuning pins
2 Capo or bearing bar
3 Strings
4 Hammers
5 Hammer rail
6 Back checks

7 Key slip
8 Plate
9 Sound-board
10 Bridges
11 Hitch pins

*I apologise for omitting Matthay's lavish capitals and unnecessary division into numbered and lettered paragraphs.

greater the *extent* of these string vibrations, the *louder* is the note. The string must therefore traverse space more *quickly* the louder the note, since the time available (in which to traverse the larger distance embraced by the more ample vibration) remains the same as for the softer note. To produce much tone, we must therefore induce *much movement* in the string. For the more quickly the string is made to move, the greater will be the distance it can traverse during the course of each complete vibration. The string is set into motion by the felt-covered end of the pianoforte mechanism – the hammer. The hammer, upon being brought into contact with the strings, *shares* its speed with the latter whilst deflecting it. Both thereupon rebound; and the hammer, falling away from the strings, leaves the latter free to continue in vibration, gradually expending the energy communicated to it, unless stopped by the damper. The hammer can therefore only communicate movement to the string during the latter's first vibration; and can only do so during the first *quarter* of such first to-and-fro movement of the strings. As the hammer *ceases to influence* the strings the very moment that sound begins, it follows that this moment *forms the conclusion and cessation* of the act of tone production; for the string cannot move quicker than it does at that moment, since it has ceased to be under the influence either of key or finger. Tone production at the pianoforte is therefore a discontinuous act; an act separate for each note; and one that ceases with the moment when silence changes into sound. Beauty in the quality of sound depends on string's vibrations tending rather toward the *simple* types of movement, than toward the *compound* forms – the resulting tone is thus less embarrassed with the harsher harmonics. This simplicity in the string's vibration that furthers beauty of tone (vibration of the string rather as a whole than in sections) depends on the *manner* in which movement is communicated to it. The *harsher* effects arise when the string is *suddenly* set in motion; whereas the more *sympathetic* effects arise only when the string is set in motion as gradually as possible.

And here is some of what Matthay has to say about the key.

The pianoforte key is a machine to facilitate the production of speed in the string. It is a compound lever, akin in principle to the see-saw. It follows that tone production can only be effected by giving motion to the key; since this forms our only means of conveying motion to the string. Energy brought to bear upon the key *ceases* to create tone the moment that the place in key-descent is reached where the hammer's motion culminates and causes sound to begin. The act itself of tone production can hence never take longer than it does in the most extreme staccatissimo. The ear appraises us of this moment more quickly than any other of our senses; hence, we must *listen* for the beginning of sound if we would have accuracy in tone production. The more *gradually* this key-speed is attained the more beautiful is the tone *character* – the fuller, more 'sympathetic' singing and carrying in its *quality*. The more *sudden* the key depression the harsher is the resulting tone quality; it may be more 'brilliant' but it will be less effective in carrying power. . . . It is futile to squeeze the key upon its bed with the object of inducing tone, since sound, if produced at all, is given off *before* the key reaches its full depression. It is almost as futile to attempt to obtain good tone by *knocking* the key, since the concussion here caused at the key surface forms *waste* of energy intended to create tone, and thus engenders *inaccuracy* in the tonal result – the actual tone obtained not corresponding to the tone intended.

It seems inevitable, when quoting Matthay, to stray into the realm of piano teaching, nor can it be doubted that some of the above statements (and restatements) are of a highly controversial nature even today, and will be hotly contested by many. In particular his thoughts on how beauty of sound depends on string vibrations being simple rather than compound, on the string being set in motion gradually for 'sympathetic' tone will be assured of a cool reception by scientific people. But, leaving aside controversy and disregarding polemics, there is enough truth in Matthay's philosophy of piano technique to make his thoughts on strings, keys and the mechanical conditions in which they operate worth our attention. The stand Matthay made, perhaps for the first time in the history of piano playing, against the barbarous hitting and pointless squeezing that so many of our less instinctively gifted brethren went in for (no doubt because they were badly instructed) also brought home the truth, at last, that not the key but the string was the point in space at which the players' movements should be directed – the key being no more than a tool ending in the hammer mechanism, a continuation of the finger which is too short to reach the string. If Matthay did nothing more than bring this truism

23

home to students and teachers alike, his life effort was not in vain.

The reader will find diagrams of the pianoforte action and all its elements. No great mental effort is needed to grasp the physical processes involved and the part the human element – body and soul – plays in bringing about these processes. I will go into details of how the pianoforte is *played* in Part Two.

The sound-board

But first let us remember that key and string, even when their interaction is considered and explained, are only two provinces of the vast continent of the pianoforte, and several other provinces remain to be explored.

The sound-board, though it concerns primarily the piano builder, tuner and technician, and the pianist only to the extent of his desire for knowledge, nevertheless deserves a quick glance, if only because of the ingenuity, industry and patience that went into creating it – the harp inside the organ, the belly of the instrument. That admirable advocate of the human belly, Menenius Agrippa, makes it into a symbol of the benevolently distributive state, but it could almost equally well serve as a symbol of what we are about to describe.

. . . I am the store-house and the shop of the whole body: But, if you remember,
I send it through the rivers of your blood,
Even to the court, the heart, to the seat, the brain,
And, through the cranks, and offices of man,
The strongest nerves, and small inferior veins,
From me receive that natural competency,
Whereby they live . . .*

The natural competency whereby the piano lives is sound, and this is radiated in the intended direction by the sound-board; without it the mere vibration of strings would create little or no audible sound.

*Coriolanus, I, i.

W. L. Sumner, in his admirable book *The Pianoforte*, gives the following excellent description of the sound-board:

Vibrating piano strings present only a small area in contact with the air, and unless their motions are communicated to a larger surface their sounds would be quite inadequate. . . . A sound-board should be sufficiently large to produce air-motions which will result in adequate volumes of sound; it should not be too large to respond as evenly as possible to notes throughout the whole range of the compass, and it must act as the final arbiter of the tone-quality by modifying and improving it, by adding its own acoustic characteristics. . . . a successful instrument must work as a harmonious, integrated whole, like the finely co-ordinated anatomical structure of a healthy living organism. The material of which the sound-board is made should transmit sound very quickly because, as far as is possible, there should be no difference in phase of soundwaves in various parts of the sound-board; otherwise the sounds in various parts of the sound-board will tend to neutralize each other. Also the material should have the property of transmitting the sounds with a minimum of absorption of their energy. All sound, in the end, is lost by being turned into heat, and it is necessary, therefore, to find a material with a low acoustic resistance. At all stages, between the finger which imparts energy to the mechanism and the sound-board which projects it, the efficiency of the processes of transmission should be maintained to the greatest degree. In other words, the piano should maintain a maximum energy-conversion rate.

It matters little whether this precious material used for making sound-boards is Rumanian pine, Canadian sitka, or Norwegian spruce, often known as Swiss pine, all of which are enumerated by the remarkably painstaking Mr Sumner. The student of the piano should be content to know that, according to another source 'the sound-board is a mass of nerves responsive to the most minute shocks'.* That brings us nearer to Menenius Agrippa and Shakespeare!

A practical fact which every piano owner should know about the sound-board is that it may crack if it is exposed to heat – especially dry heat – for a long time; close proximity to a central heating radiator, for instance, may prove fatal. A cracked sound-board is almost impossible to repair, and

*L. Nolder, *The Modern Piano*, London 1927.

very expensive to replace, and signs of deterioration will soon be noticeable in a piano so afflicted. If you love your piano, do not place it near the radiator!

The iron frame

What more should we know about our harp inside the organ? We have discussed the hammer, connected with the key which receives kinetic energy from the player's body, and which converts this into vibrational energy, passed on for distribution to the sound-board. This is done via the strings, the increased tension of which (since in the course of years of development the pitch and consequently the total tension represented by the mass of strings rose rather steeply) necessitated in its turn the introduction of the metal frame to resist this tension – and this iron frame is today an integral and standard part of the pianoforte. And so is the wrest-plank, complete with wrest – or tuning pins, well known to all piano tuners.

The outer case

It remains to mention, *en passant*, the outer case of the instrument, no part of the harp, rather of the organ, and by no means unimportant. Its usefulness extends indeed into the realm of acoustics, as it is said to act as a sort of second sound-board; for this reason, and also for appearance and style, it has received much special attention from makers throughout the ages.

The pedal

It also remains to mention, not so *en passant*, that most important tool, which looks like an extension of the piano's outer case: the pedal. In Mozart's day the mechanism regulating the lifting and replacing of the damper was placed directly under the keyboard, and was operated by the player's knee – a facility seemingly intended for infant prodigies, or people with very short legs! Today the damper is controlled by pedals: a pedal for the right foot which is connected to the damper by a metal rod and which, on being depressed, lifts the damper off the strings; another pedal for the left foot (also complete with metal rod) which shifts the whole keyboard a little to the right of the player, thus reducing the number of strings struck by the hammer from three to two. Some modern instruments have a third pedal (known as 'sostenuto' or 'sustaining' pedal) capable of sustaining isolated notes or chords while all the other notes on the keyboard are unaffected. Since the right pedal (not quite properly named 'loud' pedal) not only lifts the damper, so giving the strings the natural length of their sound duration, but also liberates the masses of harmonics or over-tones of each string, it is advisable to remember that clashes may arise between components of the same harmony if their respective rows of harmonics conflict; it is up to the player's artistic feeling to decide whether the slightly distorted sound arising from such conflict is desirable or not. The row of harmonics (or 'partials') in the example below, at least up to Nos. 7-8,

is clearly audible on the piano if one listens attentively with the damper lifted.

On the whole it is a good idea to think of the damper pedal not as something that *lengthens* the tone but rather as something that *shortens* it, because the long vibration of the string is its natural state, cut short by the damper. For those who wish for more than just the bare facts the more artistic aspects of pedalling are discussed in Chapter 7.

Key, hammer (known as 'the action'), strings, sound-board, iron frame, the outer case, pedals: this more or less completes the description of our instrument. I do not claim infallibility or one hundred per cent completeness and the expert will not find here anything very revelatory or novel. Dreary technical terms have, as much as possible, been avoided or relegated to the diagrams. Those who want more specialized information will no doubt find excellent books to supply such information. But our concern is with the practical instrumentalist who is not indifferent to the inner nature of his instrument.

Four
Equal Temperament and Tuning*
*If you hate arithmetic you are advised to skip this chapter

The pianist who does his daily stint of practising will soon come upon problems: strings will break or get out of tune, unequal pitch conditions within a trichord will result in intolerable 'beating', to say nothing of other mechanical defects that piano actions are heirs to. It is advisable that the pianist should prepare himself, as much as possible, to act competently in an emergency when no professional tuner is within reach; discounting any intervention outside the scope of the mechanically untrained, I propose to give a very brief outline of what every pianist ought to know about piano tuning. It is not very difficult – all that is needed is a good ear, a tuning hammer and a piece of felt.

It is unfair to say that any violinist can put us to shame. The violinist's job is simple; he has only four strings which he tunes, relying entirely on his hearing, in pure fifths – any adjustments that may become necessary in the course of the performance, or, to put it more accurately, any deviations from absolute purity, are matters of intonation, of judging correctly the point at which his finger touches the string. For deviations from absolute purity are necessary when our violinist makes music in which a piano also plays a part, or even in an orchestra sometimes, as explained in Chapter 11.

Anyone who ever attempted to tune all seven octaves of a piano 'by ear' will have suffered the most gruesome experience of his life: despite his excellent ear and the best of intentions, the result will be an unbearable jumble in which nothing sounds right. Why does this happen? Science gives the following answer: our tonal system, under which the octave is divided into twelve semitones, if not exactly arbitrary, is

29

nevertheless a compromise system, the laws of nature being slightly bent in favour of something more suitable to our needs.

It is not necessary to go into the question of consonance and dissonance to understand this. We have come a long way since Pythagoras proclaimed that 'all nature consists of harmony arising out of number'. Nor can we accept from Euler that the human mind delights in law and order and therefore takes more pleasure in intervals whose ratio frequencies can be expressed by small numbers (the consonances); our ears have, in hundreds of years, become so conditioned to dissonance that we no longer hear it as dissonance, and have neither pleasure nor displeasure in consonance. It is possible that Helmholtz hit the nail on the head when he explained consonance and dissonance in terms of conflict or agreement between the respective harmonics of the notes in question. This has some bearing on our subject.

Expressed in terms of simple arithmetic, the problem of temperament is as follows: The ratio of frequency (vibration rate per second) of any note and its octave is 2, that of seven octaves 2^7. Seven octaves equal twelve fifths. The frequency ratio of a 'pure' fifth is $\frac{3}{2}$ and of twelve fifths $(\frac{3}{2})^{12}$. This is more than 2^7. Thus if we proceed from the bottom C of the pianoforte to the top one in pure fifths we ultimately arrive at a C which has a slightly higher frequency than that of C. This is known as the 'Pythagorean comma' and is rather less than a quarter of a semitone.

To make this even clearer, I will quote from Sir James Jeans's *Science and Music*. The author uses a clock-face showing the twelve intervals (fifths) making the full circle from C to C to illustrate his meaning.

. . . the 'comma of Pythagoras' is distributed equally over the twelve intervals which make up the circle on the clock-face. As the comma is about a quarter of a semitone, this involves flattening each interval of a fifth by about a forty-eighth of a semitone. Or, to be more precise, since the twelve steps round the clock-face are to represent an interval of exactly seven octaves, and so a frequency ratio of 128:1, each step must represent a frequency ratio of

$\dfrac{12}{\sqrt{128}}$ or 1·4983. All semitones are now equal and . . . each represents precisely the same frequency ratio, 1·0587.

The figures are different, the meaning is the same: only the octaves are strictly in tune. Because, if all the fifths are slightly flattened in order to make the octaves pure and to arrive on a top C which is the 'same' note as the bottom C (a procedure known as 'distributing the Pythagorean comma'), other intervals will suffer the repercussions of this: the fourths will have to be slightly wide, the thirds quite wide, and the minor sixths equivalently narrow.

It is not certain whether Bach's 'Well-tempered Clavier' was based on the 'equal temperament' idea or on the so-called 'mean tone' temperament (where the major thirds are in tune, the fifth slightly narrow, and the differences between major and minor seconds 'smoothed out'), or some sort of mixture of the two; but, since it is obvious that without some kind of temperature it was impossible to play 'in tune' in all the keys – and Bach's great keyboard work, using all twenty-four tonalities, was designed to prove that, given his new system of tuning, this was now possible – it follows that Bach's system was most probably the forerunner of ours, at least in principle if not in all details. In that case he was a great scientist as well as perhaps the greatest of all musicians.

It has been suggested that if, instead of dividing the octave by twelve semitones, we adopted a scale of fifty-three tones (in which notes like C sharp and D flat would be represented by separate keys giving them their true pitch) that would solve all our problems. Yes, if such a keyboard would be playable by human hands. But, as Sir James Jeans himself admits, '. . . our limited scales have their origin in the limitation of our hands'.

When playing in concert with orchestra or with single instruments in chamber music, problems connected with the piano's equal temperament will arise. I have not touched on this in Chapter 11 (the piano combined with other instruments) because the problems are largely problems of intonation for the other instrument, or instruments – the pianist can do nothing to solve them. Such adjustments of intonation (in the high frequencies in particular) become necessary in purely orchestral performance also – without keyboard instrument – and a really sharp-eared conductor should demand them.

International standard pitch (fixed in 1939) is A = 440, which means 440 complete vibrations per second for the A above middle C, at 60 degrees Fahrenheit. The temperature (heat) co-efficient affects other instruments more than it affects the piano, which stays in tune a reasonably long time.

For an accurate and painstaking description of the act of tuning let us turn once again to W. L. Sumner, for I can hardly improve upon his effort.

The tuner may begin with the note A above middle C. By means of wedges or dampers the centre and right hand strings of the trichord* are silenced and the left hand string is brought up to the pitch of the tuning fork, A = 440, so that no beats are heard. The tuning lever is usually known as the tuning hammer, and its star-shaped aperture fits neatly over the wrest-pin. If the fullest leverage allowed by the tuning hammer is used a better control of the motion of the wrest-pin and less fatigue of the hand will result. The tuning hammer should fit easily on the pin and care should be taken to see that only a turn and not a lateral motion, which would tend to bend the pin, is given to it. Good tuners quickly sense the feel of the pin and tend to bring the string slightly above pitch and then 'spring the pin', that is to say, allow the tensional strain on it to twist out. During tuning the keys should be struck with reasonable force so that subsequent heavy playing does not quickly cause the note to go flat. Then the central string is tuned to its neighbour while the third is muted and finally the third string is brought into true pitch with the other two. Forcible, but never brutal, testing of the note should show that the three strings are in tune with one another and that there is no sign of beating. The A, an octave below, is now tuned by damping with wedges two of its strings and tuning the left-hand string to be the true sub-octave of the first A to be tuned. Some very experienced tuners narrow the octave by an extraordinarily small amount and hardly enough to make its presence felt as beats before the notes die away. In any case, any slight widening of this octave is fatal to subsequent

*Trichord means the three strings tuned to each note.

tuning. The next note to be tuned is the E above this lower A. This interval, like all other fifths, must be slightly narrow, and beats should be listened for, between harmonics of the two notes. Musicians who have a good sense of relative pitch often need practice for weeks before they can detect and estimate the frequency of the beats. This E may be tested by its beating with the first A to be tuned. . . . The beats of fourths are somewhat quicker than those of fifths in the same part of the scale. The octave below E is then tuned, and some advanced tuners will tune this octave very slightly narrow. The fifth B above this, then F♯ a fifth above are tuned and so on. . . . F♯ may be tested against A for it will produce the characteristic sound of the tempered sixth, which should become familiar to the ear by repeatedly listening to sixths played on a well-tuned instrument. When C♯ has been tuned the A major chord may be tried and should yield a fully satisfying sound. As the process of fixing the pitches, known as 'laying the bearings', proceeds, tests with various sixths may be made. Tempered tenths are more easy to listen to than thirds, and their particular type of sound should become familiar to the ear. When the tuning proceeds downwards and G♯ becomes available, the E major chord may be played and savoured. As thirds and sixths become available, they should be tested. The last octave is the downward G and the final note is the D above this, which should be tested as a slightly narrow fifth against the first A to be tuned. This method of laying the bearings is known as tuning the great circle of fifths. Another method, using fourths and fifths is given in the diagram, and this does not exhaust the possibilities. The upper and lower notes of the scale are then tuned as octaves.

Tuning (top) in fifths and octaves

Tuning (lower) in fourths and fifths

Here it is, then, in the proverbial nutshell. Those who care should read this chapter with attention, for they will in time derive pleasure from what their new-found knowledge yields them in terms of practical advantage. But I would not be surprised to learn that only a small minority cares.

Five
A Little Bit of History

God created the violin on the first day of creation, and it has remained virtually unchanged ever since. Not so the piano. This complex system of variously constructed mechanisms has needed some three hundred years of evolution to reach its present form; and who knows if the instrument we call the pianoforte really represents the end of this evolution, or if future composers will have something of even greater perfection to write their music for?

Ignore the earliest origins. Ignore the one-string monochord, the four-string helikon, or the quaintly named 'exaquir', or 'esquaquiel', or even 'echiquier d'Angleterre', a kind of stringed organ. They all belong to the limbo in which historians like to browse. Ignore also the 'hackbrett', a seventeenth-century relation of the Hungarian gypsies' 'cimbalom'; the inventor of this instrument, by the remarkable name of Pantaleon Hebenstreit, presented it to Louis XIV of France, who named it, after its inventor, 'Pantalon'.

Our interest surely begins to be roused when the instrument, no longer a mere machine to make sound, becomes a means of creating, or recreating, Art. We are somewhat restricted by the fact that the charming and interesting forerunners of our instrument, which go by the names harpsichord, clavichord, virginal and the like, will be dealt with by another book in the present series; disregarding them, and the very highly cultured period they symbolize, is not to disregard significant links with our period and our instrument (which must become obvious to readers of both books), but merely a concession made to the necessity of a clear line of demarcation between one cultural period and another. Of course

35

such clear divisions do not, in fact, exist, as every historian knows, but they are postulated here for the sake of easier practical application.

The pianoforte, an instrument fitted with hammers and capable of producing soft (piano) and loud (forte) sound at the player's will, was not a German invention as was believed by Beethoven, who insisted on calling it by a German name, '*Hammerclavier*'. The man who had the idea of substituting hammers for the harpsichord jacks was an Italian, Bartolomeo Cristofori (1650-1731), and this epoch-making idea is still the essential constant factor today, perhaps the only thing about the pianoforte which centuries of change have hardly touched.

Cristofori was later accused of stealing the invention by a German music teacher called Gottfried Schröder, who claimed that it was his. Nevertheless there seems little doubt that Cristofori was the original inventor. He held a position to one of the Medici princes not unlike that of the British 'Master of the Queen's Musick', and had access to every kind of instrument for his experiments. According to W. L. Sumner, Cristofori had, by the year of 1726, so improved his pianoforte action that it had all the vital elements of a modern action (double lever, escapement, check, and even the 'una corda' mechanism) and, according to the same authority, a composer called Giustini di Pistoia composed the first music, twelve sonatas, for the new instrument, at about the time of Cristofori's death.

The next important step – and this takes us into the period 1770-1830, when Mozart and Beethoven were composing – was the re-thinking, on the part of the piano makers, of the notion that the pianoforte was a harpsichord with hammers instead of plectra. It took some time to realize that it was a new instrument, in terms of thickness, heaviness, tension of strings and resistance to tension. Gottfried Silbermann (1683-1753) made two pianos and submitted them to the great Bach. We are told that the great man took an entirely negative view of the merits of the new instrument, then still in

36

need of improvement. But the following quote from Bach's pupil, J. F. Agricola, tells a somewhat different story.

. . . Mr Gottfried Silbermann had at first built two of these instruments. One of them was seen and played by the late Kapellmeister, Mr Joh. Sebastian Bach. He had praised, indeed admired, its tone; but he had complained that it was too weak in the high register, and was too hard to play. This had been taken greatly amiss by Mr Silbermann who could not bear to have any fault found in his handiworks. He was therefore angry at Mr Bach for a long time. And yet his conscience told him that Mr Bach was not wrong. He therefore decided – greatly to his credit be it said – not to deliver any more of these instruments, but instead to think all the harder about how to eliminate the faults Mr J. S. Bach had observed. He worked for many years on this. And that this was the real cause of this postponement I have the less doubt since I myself heard it frankly acknowledged by Mr Silbermann. Finally, when Mr Silbermann had really achieved many improvements, notably in respect to the action, he sold one again to the Court of the Prince of Rudolstadt. . . . Mr Silbermann had also had the laudable ambition to show one of these instruments of his later workmanship to the late Kapellmeister Bach, and had it examined by him, and he had received, in turn, complete approval from him.*

Arthur Loesser, in his social history called *Men, Women and Pianos*, ventures the opinion that the sixty-two-year-old master was merely being polite, and was not going to learn new tricks – he did not, in fact, show any further interest in the pianoforte.

By this time it must be fairly obvious that the new instrument, its potentialities at last recognized by craftsmen anxious to devise improvements, had migrated from its native land, Italy, to Germany and thence to England. From now on the scene of further progress was laid in these countries, France joining in somewhat later. Italy, essentially a country of vocal culture and operatic productivity, seems to have lost interest in the pianoforte – a state of things which, oddly enough, has persisted into our present age. No competitive pianoforte has ever come out of Italy, the country where it originated.

*From *A Treatise on the Organ and Other Instruments* (1768), quoted by W. L. Sumner.

By the end of the eighteenth century a crystallization process took place in which it became possible to distinguish the basic differences in the principles on which the various actions were founded. The Viennese or German was a single action in which the hammer was mounted on the key itself. This (according to Sumner) achieved perfection around 1780. It was reputed to have easy repetition action, lighter and shallower touch than the so-called English action, as well as better balance between bass and treble. While it apparently did little to improve on Cristofori, it had, at any rate, a good damping system which pleased Mozart. Devised by Andreas Stein (1728-92), who was a pupil of Silbermann and an organ builder, and whose daughter Nannette, married to one Andreas Streicher of Vienna, continued (together with her husband) her father's work, this piano was noted for its greater beauty of sound compared with the modern iron-framed piano.

Another figure deserving of mention was Johannes Zumpe, one of G. Silbermann's workmen who came to England around 1756 to escape troubles caused in Germany by the Seven Years' War, who made mostly small square pianos slightly resembling clavichords. The weakness of these instruments (of which one or two still exist in England) was that the hammers, when hit forcefully, were apt to strike the strings more than once. Nevertheless J. C. Bach – the London-based son of the great J. S. – gave a recital on a Zumpe pianoforte in 1768.

Let us hear what Mozart had to say about the Stein piano:

This time I shall begin at once with Stein's pianofortes. Before I had seen any of his make, Späth's claviers had always been my favourites. But now I much prefer Stein's, for they damp ever so much better than the Regensburg instruments. When I strike hard, I can keep my finger on the note or raise it, but the sound ceases the moment I have produced it. In whatever way I touch the keys, the tone is always even. It never jars, it is never stronger or weaker or entirely absent; in a word, it is always even. It is true that he does not sell a pianoforte of this kind for less than 300 Gulden, but the trouble and the labour that Stein puts into the making of it cannot be paid for. His instruments have this splendid advantage over others, that they are made with escape action. Only one maker in a hundred bothers about this. But without an escapement it is impossible to avoid jangling and vibration after the note is struck. When you touch the keys, the hammers fall back again the moment after they have struck the strings, whether you hold down the keys or release them. He himself told me that when he has finished making one of these claviers, he sits down to it and tries all kinds of passages, runs and jumps, and he polishes and works away at it until it can do anything. For he labours solely in the interest of music and not for his own profit: otherwise he would soon finish his work. He often says: 'If I were not myself such a passionate lover of music, and had not myself some slight skill on the clavier, I should certainly long ago have lost patience with my work. But I do like an instrument which never lets the player down and which is durable.' And his claviers certainly do last. He guarantees that the sounding-board will neither break nor split. When he has finished making one for a clavier, he places it in the open air, exposing it to rain, snow, the heat of the sun and all the devils in order that it may crack. Then he inserts wedges and glues them in to make the instrument very strong and firm. He is delighted when it cracks, for he can be sure that nothing more can happen to it. Indeed he often cuts into it himself and then glues it together again and strengthens it in this way. . . . The device, too, which you work with your knee, is better on this than on other instruments.* I have only to touch it and it works; and when you shift your knee the slightest bit, you do not feel the least reverberation.†

There could hardly be a more expert or more sharply observant comment on the Stein piano – the finest example, perhaps, of the Viennese action – than Mozart's. One would wish that our present-day pianists and composers knew, or cared, as much about the inside workings of our modern piano.

We have no comparable document extolling the qualities of the so-called English action – perhaps because it still had a long way to go to achieve perfection, whereas the Viennese action made no further progress but gradually disappeared from the scene. The famous pianist and composer Hummel was critical of both the Viennese and the English actions: in the English action he found 'greater durability and fullness

*The knee device worked the sustaining mechanism; in England this was done by pedal.
†From a letter by Mozart to his father, 1777; translation by Emily Anderson.

of tone', but less 'facility of execution'; he says 'the touch is heavier, the key sinks much deeper, and, consequently, the return of the hammer upon the repetition of a note cannot take place so quickly . . .'.

Interesting, how points of view change: Mozart liked Stein's damping because of the precision it possessed in cutting the sound short, while we in this age concentrate on the opposite – on how to prolong sound; Hummel preferred shallow key-depression, whereas today almost every pianist feels the need of a resistant key which does not reach its bed too quickly. Kalkbrenner however praises the 'larger style and beautiful way of singing' on the English piano.

Perhaps it is justified to assume that Mozart used the 'knee device' sparingly, whereas the Clementi School of pianists, on English instruments, introduced a more modern way of using it, freely, in accordance with harmonic progressions. More will be said about Clementi and Field in Part Three.

To sum up, the English action is the true continuation of the design Cristofori invented. It is a so-called double action as against the German (Viennese) single action. This is how W. L. Sumner describes it:

The double lever multiplied both the speed and the distance of the descent of the key by a large factor. . . . The escapement allowed good repetition and the check prevented it from bouncing. . . . Piano makers were slow to improve on Cristofori's mechanism, but it became the basis of the actions of the larger concert pianofortes of the nineteenth century, and improvements in design, materials, and methods of manufacture have resulted in the robust, reliable yet sensitive actions of the modern pianoforte.

By this time, of course, the iron frame had become an integral part of the instrument, which started an inevitable process of growth in every direction to meet the demand for bigger volume of sound which must have come from the Beethoven type of composer. Also towards the *fin-de-siècle* the pianoforte started ousting its older rival, the harpsichord, from public favour, a process that was complete by 1800. The leading firm of harpsichord makers at the time, named Kirkman, tried to resist the change: they gave away harpsichords to girls who would play them in the streets of London. Eventually they capitulated and were absorbed by the piano firm of Collard & Collard, a firm founded by no less a person than Muzio Clementi. The British firm of Broadwood deserves to be mentioned here: they made Beethoven's famous 'Hammerclavier', and presented it to the master.

If the eighteenth-century part of the great pianoforte adventure was mostly enacted in Germany and England, the nineteenth century saw the significant entry into the arena of France, in the person of Sebastien Erard (1752-1831). One of the greatest instrument makers the world has ever seen, he not only devised the basis of all subsequent piano actions but also left his mark on the history of the harp and the organ. Erard constructed his first pianoforte in 1777, in the château of the Duchesse de Villeroi.

Great events of history impinged on pianoforte making, and they seem to have had the effect of driving a number of important protagonists of the piano craft from their own countries to peaceful England where they could continue their work, much to the ultimate profit and advantage of the host country. Thus as Zumpe had flown from the horrors of the Seven Years' War, the French Revolution made Sebastien Erard come to England where he started a factory in Great Marlborough Street, London, and 1796 saw the birth of the first Erard 'grand', with an improved English action. In 1821 the epoch-making 'double escapement' action was completed and a patent was taken out in England by Sebastien's nephew Pierre Erard. The main advantage of the new invention was that it permitted easy and almost unlimited speed in repetition of a note. The famous pianist Moscheles, a friend of Beethoven's, wrote:

Pierre Erard showed and explained to me. . . his uncle Sebastien's near completed invention. It consists in the key, when only sunk halfway, again rising and repeating the note. I was the first to play upon one of the newly completed instruments, and found it of priceless value for the repetition of notes.

Erard had to suffer some persecution, even in England, presumably from envious competitors, but he was eventually protected and vindicated when the Privy Council had heard much evidence in his favour.

His inventions, made in response to greater and greater demands on the piano from composers after Beethoven in the matter of volume, ease of execution and sustaining power, represent the terminal stage of a long process of evolution. After this there will be still bigger and better pianos, improvements will take place in the quality of the material, many details in the instrument will have to keep pace with a more and more critical public demand. But basically the history of the pianoforte spans what happened from the time Cristofori thought of using hammers instead of plectra, until the time Erard invented the double escapement.

Whether or not we look upon our own twentieth century as an Age of Fulfilment, an age of reaping and enjoying what our forefathers had sown, depends on each individual's temperament, on the way he reacts to the world we live in. Perhaps it is early days, perhaps a revolution in pianoforte making is yet to come, perhaps this is not the time to make up the final reckonings – who knows?

There is no doubt that experiments to make the pianoforte a 'legato' instrument from a 'staccato' one have not met with success, and can be briefly dismissed. The so-called '*Nüremberg Geigenwerk*', an early attempt at bowing the strings with circular bows worked by treadles, a similar thing called the 'clavirol', made by John Isaac Hawkins of Philadelphia, another type which imitated the vibrato (*Bebung*) of the clavichord, yet another method which employed currents of air to keep the strings vibrating – they all came and went without creating too much of a stir, as did all the debasing and absurd pedal devices imitating drums, cymbals and the like. A different kind of reform – that of easier handling – was attempted by an inventor called Clutsam, who devised a circular keyboard which embodied keys of different sizes; and the Hungarian Emanuel Moor invented a pianoforte with two manuals which could be coupled (harpsichord fashion) for easy octave playing and which had, between the two manuals, a tier where black and white keys were on one level, for chromatic glissando. Alas the coupled octaves did not make the same sound as the ones played by hand, the chromatic glissando turned out to be a white elephant (or should one say, a black-and-white elephant?) – nobody wanted it – and some disadvantages of a rather heavy action discouraged pianists from spending years learning to play an instrument for which no music existed. The Moor piano, after a few years of attracting attention, went out, along with other contemporary gadgets.

Another Hungarian, P. von Janko, slightly anticipating Moor, surprised the world with a 'terrace' model which sported six keyboards placed on top of each other, forming one single chromatic scale. Its aim was easier stretches and the possibility of novel effects, but this also proved to be a nine days' wonder, or something even more ephemeral.

Mention must be made, however, of the fact that in this twentieth century America made an important, indeed decisive, appearance in the pianoforte world. This was largely due to the Steinway family – Germans originally called by the name of Steinweg. World events, as we have seen, played an important part in directing forces destined to shape the future of the pianoforte from one part of the world to another, just as the Seven Years' War made the German piano maker Zumpe come to England, just as the French Revolution brought Sebastien Erard out of France and, again, into England, this time it was the 1848 revolution that propelled the Steinwegs from Germany to the Promised Land, the United States of America. Henry Engelhard Steinweg (later Steinway), described by Theodore E. Steinway in his little book *People and Pianos* as 'strong-willed, sturdy and courageous', was born in 1797 and died in 1871. His life was in every sense a bridge – from the eighteenth to the nineteenth, and, through his descendants, well into the twentieth century, from the old world to the new. The Steinway piano embodies the Erard action, improved and perfected, the so-called over-strung

43

scale, the middle (sustaining) pedal, about eighteen other patented improvements, and is today considered the nearest thing to perfection that it is possible for a pianoforte to be. C. F. Theodore Steinway's German motto is:

Geselle ist wer was kann;
Meister ist wer was ersann;
Lehrling ist jedermann.

Who knows his trade is a journey man;
A master is he who invents the plan;
An apprentice, each and every man.

Other American firms, no less excellent in their results, like Chickering, Knabe, Baldwin, Mason & Hamlin etc., have nevertheless found it impossible to withstand the merciless competition engendered by American commercialism, and all except Baldwin have gone out of business.

America's triumphant entry on the scene of piano making did not mean any decline of the standard of European-made instruments – quite the contrary. The Viennese firm of Bösendorfer makes beautiful mellow-toned pianos (extolled by Liszt, Backhaus and others). The Germans, represented by Bechstein, Blüthner (who invented the so-called 'aliquot' strings, a set of extra strings placed above the highest register to add brilliance to the sound), Grotrian Steinweg, the French maker Pleyel, all these make marvellous instruments. They differ only slightly from each other in the matter of heaviness or lightness of action, and a few details of construction.

And what of the future? It is usually the creative musicians, the composers, who inspire piano makers with new ideas. Our electronic age has so far failed to do so. We can but wait and hope.

Part Two:

Playing the Piano

Six
Aspects of Technique*
*What follows is mostly practical advice: no one should expect infallibility, comprehensiveness – or a 'method'

Seat and connected topics

When you say to a pupil 'seat yourself at the piano', you are not always aware that you have posed a problem. 'How shall I sit?' asks the unfortunate pupil. 'High or low or somewhere in between? Should my back be straight, and my arm bent in the elbow joint at right angles? And where do I place my feet and legs?' These and other similar questions torment pupils and teachers alike, and many methods have many different answers. But let us be patient and accept the fact that for different individuals all the conflicting answers could be right, or at least have *something* good in them.

No teacher ought to force his pupil to become, even in his physical attitudes, a copy of his master, but allow him to follow his own instinct. If the pupil has long legs and a long body, his natural inclination will be to sit lower than his shorter built colleague, and the length of his arms will at least influence, if not determine, the distance at which he will like to sit from the keyboard. In the long run the teacher should only act as a moderating influence if excessive wrongdoing, caused by lack of experience, is blatantly obvious. Some young persons, misled by the fallacy that a very high seat enables you to 'hit' the key from greater distance and therefore more strongly, will adjust their stool as high as it will go, adding books, cushions and what not – and at this stage it might well be advisable to point out that hitting the keys (even the right keys!) is not the end of piano technique.

Sit at a moderate height, and a moderate distance, such that will give you a sensation of comfort, ease and relaxation

47

in your whole body. Your stretched-out arm should just about reach the black keys, your upper body, diaphragm relaxed and round-shouldered, should be able to bend forwards, backwards and sideways. You should get used quite early on to a natural position of the arms, neither bent at right angles, nor stretched out at 180 degrees, for these positions are rarely required in piano playing. The obtuse angle, with adequate freedom of movement in all directions, could be adopted as normal. Your right foot should be placed on the right pedal (even when this is not in use). But as it is an abuse to use the 'soft' pedal every time you wish to play softly, your left foot should not live on the left pedal, nor should it be used for beating time. And your left leg should not be curled, ivy-fashion, round the leg of the stool – but rather pulled backwards a bit and used to lean on. Sometimes this left leg carries the weight of your whole body, and therefore the tip-toe fashion favoured by some younger pupils is not advisable. It is better to sit lightly on the stool, not too far back, not heavily slumped, but elastically 'at the ready'.

I myself favour the low seat, but claim no specific reason, other than build, physical habit and feeling of comfort. If one's technique is based on the 'leverage' idea rather than on direct force brought to bear on the keyboard, then the sensations in the act of playing will be *upward* sensations rather than *downward* ones, and for this the low seat is more favourable. Pianists who, by reason of early training or physical build, favour the active application of physical force, will prefer to sit higher. According to Breithaupt Liszt preferred a low seat, but the Russian professor Milstein denies that there is any truth in this. Paderewski sat low, Rachmaninov medium low, and Busoni rather high, while some of the present-day young generation favour very high seats. Clearly no conclusions can be drawn about a pianist's technique from the height of his seat.

Altogether it is dangerous to put down cut-and-dried rules about technique. I have heard pianists who had 'impossible' hands which looked half crippled on the keyboard, and who did all the things condemned by almost everybody else, per-

48

Plate 4. Hand carving the case of a Louis XV grand.

Plate 5. 'Voicing' the piano – that is, treating the hammers to ensure proper tone quality – depends largely on the ear and judgement of the regulator.

↓ 5

form miracles of technical perfection. In matters of piano technique so much depends on imagination, temperament and imponderable things of the mind, and genius often proves that the impossible is the only right solution – in short in Art there can be no categorical rules and no simple solutions.

Muscular freedom

Passive or active, the sensation of freedom from muscular strain in the arm, especially in the elbow, should be cultivated early on. This should be easy with children (who are naturally relaxed) but not so easy with adults or adolescents who have already acquired bad muscular habits. The civilized life in the western hemisphere tends to disregard the training of the human body to perform everyday muscular functions without losing its original elasticity. Either this is done more intelligently in the east, or the eastern races, born with more pliable musculature, resist the corrupting influence of schools and athletic exercises more successfully. Practically every adolescent pupil from England, America and most parts of Europe has to be painstakingly taught to relax his or her muscles; those coming from the east do this naturally, almost automatically. This is not to say, of course, that eastern people are more musically gifted, only easier to teach, as any practitioner of the art of piano teaching will confirm.

The 'piano hand'

The essential requirements of a good pianistic hand proved a constant source of contention among past generations of piano teachers. The relative value of long or short fingers, a broad, fleshy hand or a slender bony one were topics for constant discussion until it was realized that it was not in the shape of the hand but in the mind directing its actions that the battle was lost or won. As I said before, the most improbable hands can occasionally perform feats of virtuosity that are denied to some more likely-looking ones, simply through force

Plate 6. Hand sanding and finishing the ribs (underside) of a concert grand sound-board.
Plate 7. Glueing the support flange to the support.

of mind, that rare combination of imagination and concentration (the former for the design, the latter for the execution) which characterizes the artist. A seemingly unsuitable hand can be transformed, by intense exercising, into a suitable one, and stretches of an octave and more, impossible at first, can become easy, sometimes in a matter of months. Teachers in this day and age know how to treat the too chubby, too flabby hands of young girls and boys, how to widen the sometimes too narrow gaps between fingers, how to get rid of monstrous habits like bending fingers outwards, how to transform double-jointed thumbs from liabilities into assets. Only the hard, inflexible, bony hand, with unyielding sinews and no natural mobility of the fingers, may at times prove an insurmountable obstacle even to the most persistent lover of music – in such a case you have to accept failure. But it is not often that real talent is so fatally inhibited; as a rule it possesses the right pair of hands from the start, or has a potential to be developed in the course of study.

As for the length of fingers, it is a well-known fact that amongst the famous pianists of the past a roughly equal number belonged to the long-finger and the short-finger group respectively. Busoni, Rachmaninov, Rosenthal, Sauer, had long fingers; d'Albert, Reisenauer, Teresa Carreño, Pachmann and others had short ones. Liszt's fingers were not exceptionally long (contemporary legends notwithstanding) but had the advantage of very deep-lying connective tissues between them, giving them an unusual degree of independence. But too much importance should not be attached to the shape, strength and general efficiency of the hands, and attempts to improve them (instead of the mind of the player) can lead to damaging results. Everyone knows how Schumann ruined his hand by trying to make his fingers more 'independent'. And what a loss for the world it would have been if the great teacher Leschetizky had sent young Paderewski packing because he had unsuitable hands!

There are plenty of useful exercises which aim at restoring still young muscles to their original state of elasticity. 'Elasticity' is perhaps a better word than 'relaxation', which is an inaccurate oversimplification when applied to piano playing. One exercise meant to remove rigidity entails throwing the resting arm from one's lap on to the keyboard. In another the teacher's hand, supporting the pupil's arm, is suddenly taken away to test if the arm then drops downwards, which it will do if relaxed. Such exercises should be practised by beginners before any actual playing is attempted. But it should be borne in mind that muscles which are soft and relaxed during exercises will contract and stiffen when attention is deflected by the musical exploration of the keyboard which sooner or later has to take the place of pure relaxation exercises.

The position while playing

So you have settled to your own satisfaction the question of seat (high or low), and the question of what the arms, feet, legs and body should – and perhaps more important, should *not* – do. But the next question is: what happens when you start to play? How will the many acts involved in the act of playing affect the limbs concerned, what will your arms and legs look like, how will they behave in the course of a coherent performance? Is it important or unimportant, useful or useless, to stick to a 'basic position' with regard to the height of the wrist, the height to which the fingers are raised and the angle of the hand and forearm relative to the keyboard – again all questions that furnished generations of teachers and theorists endless material for controversy.

Simple common sense answers: of course there can be no static position throughout the performance. Neither the wrist (which should be free to undulate up and down and rotate to either side), nor the hand can possibly be kept motionless, as teachers of a hundred years ago demanded of their pupils. I can think of nothing more horrifying in the way of misguided teachers' zeal than the trick of placing a coin between the knuckles of the hand while the unfortunate pupil had to play without displacing or losing the coin – or else. Absurd as this may sound to the present generation, I can vouch for the

51

fact that the 'coin method' was practised even in my own lifetime. Of course hand, wrist, forearm, upper arm, fingers, even the body are in constant motion. At most, if a tendency towards excessive body and head movement is strikingly noticeable in a pupil's demeanour, the teacher should intervene with a recommendation of greater discipline. The same applies to other bad habits, like singing, snorting, making hideous faces, stertorous breathing and the like. (But the treatment of such infantile failings ought not to be too harsh: they come into the category of 'leaks', that is to say surplus emotion directed into the wrong channel by nervousness, and should disappear in the course of time. Where such leakages persist past adolescence they should be dealt with vigorously by the teacher, or the afflicted person himself, if he or she has the necessary will-power.)

Breathing

It is a good idea to learn early on the value and practice of regular breathing, preferably through the diaphragm, as singers do, and not through the open mouth. Holding your breath causes not only discomfort, but mistakes in your playing; 'wrong notes' and even memory faults can be the result of bad breathing technique and the related fault of stiffening the stomach muscles. Involuntary little muscular convulsions can easily happen in any part of the body, with unfavourable effect on playing efficiency, and these should be carefully watched in the early stages and, as much as possible, eliminated.

Fingers

Outmoded techniques. All teachers, past and present, were and are aware of the fact that the finger, even the heaviest finger, is not heavy enough to overcome the resistance of the key in our modern pianoforte action by its weight alone. You can easily try this out by dropping your raised finger, without muscular action, on to the key: no sound will result.

The old, now outmoded, method to overcome this difficulty was strenuous finger training: this made the fingers as strong as it is possible for such comparatively small and muscularly not over-endowed limbs to be. There were also further athletic exercises with the absurd aim of making the fingers not only 'strong' but also 'independent' – something that is manifestly impossible by reason of an anatomical arrangement of nature (an arrangement that has great practical advantages) under which the fingers of the hand are, to a varying extent, interdependent. It is not necessary to know anatomy to appreciate this: a simple test will prove that movement by any one finger will excite sympathetic co-movement in another, or several others, and while it is possible to reduce this to a reasonable minimum, it would be foolish to try to eliminate it by so-called 'shackling' exercises or by mechanical means.

Many a young pianist was crippled by these methods: over-muscled in the wrong places, subject to painful inflammation in the tendons and muscles, inhibited in the matter of tone production (where he could only achieve a harsh-sounding fortissimo and an almost inaudible anaemic kind of pianissimo). Such a young pianist had to possess really outstanding talent to survive, artistically speaking, and find his own way, through trial and error, to a serviceable technique. On the other hand it must be admitted that if he did so survive, he at least had at his disposal the strong athletic fingers cultivated by this old method. To such a case applies the saying 'What does not kill me, makes me stronger'. But these survivors, few in number, do not really prove the excellence of the method as such, only the strength of their own talent.

The late Artur Schnabel, perhaps himself such a victim, used to declare that it did not matter in the least how a pupil was taught: he would grow up and fashion his own technique, according to his own personality. No doubt this is true. But what hard, stone-breaking work, how many false starts, what desperation can be saved the young person by the understanding teacher who knows his job, and who does, after all, nothing more than show the pupil his own way to himself!

After the old finger-raising school, and partly coinciding with it, came what was once called the 'weight' method: the facts of life, such as the usefulness of relaxation and of using the stronger muscles of shoulder and upper arm, were discovered. It is only natural that this should have been slightly over-worked – all new ideas, however sound in themselves, suffer that fate. The books about weight technique are full of anatomical details, terms like 'pronation', 'supination', 'abduction' and 'adduction', all relating to different ways of using one's arms and shoulders; no wonder the authors of these works had little time for mere fingers, and the so-called 'fingerlessness' of some of their pupils bears witness to the way a basically good idea can have disastrous results. I myself have come across one or two 'fingerless' pupils and have reluctantly come to the conclusion that this might be a worse failing (because more difficult to cure) than the old-fashioned 'fingers-only' fallacy.

The contemporary approach. Surely the first principle of a good technique must be to play the cards that nature has dealt us in the best possible way and to the greatest possible advantage without breaking the rules of the game by force. Or, if you prefer the metaphor, we need not jump over our obstacles as in a horse race since we are allowed to choose another way around them. Working on this principle, independence of the fingers can be achieved, in effect if not in a physiological sense, by allowing the arm to follow its natural inclination to roll, rotate, swing or circle, thereby bringing each finger in turn to a vertical position above the key or keys required; this vertical position of each finger in relation to each key is the nearest nature allows us to get to independence of fingers.

The thumb. Oddly enough, the finger with the biggest share of independence, the thumb, is less frequently used for its mobility – it can both move sideways and rotate, unlike the other fingers – than for its strength in lending the other fingers a secure base to operate from, something akin to a 'fulcrum'. This seems a pity; the thumb (which, incidentally, touches the key with its side, not its tip) is too often held well away from the hand and thus immobilized. But it is in playing scales and passages that the thumb's importance in changing position becomes very evident: then it is moved from the 'away' position towards the key which will be its next landing place. This move – which should be gradual, not sudden – is carried out under cover of the rest of the fingers or the upper surface of the hand, and is almost invisible; the thumb travels, almost hidden, between the palm and the key until it is time to sound its next note. This process remains much the same whether the direction of the passage is upwards or downwards on the keyboard.

It is easy to see that more than just a movement of the thumb is necessary to carry out this displacement of the thumb, or to 'change position', the requirements of such displacement being smoothness and the absence of any bumps or accents. Here the rotating faculty of the arm must be used. Modern teaching is a little divided on this.

Matthay recommends a wrist-forearm movement which, in going upwards on the keyboard, tilts the angle of the hand to the keyboard a little to the left; this shortens and facilitates the thumb movement, after which the hand returns to its former angle. For the left hand read 'right' instead of 'left'. This may work for some pianists, but it seems a bit cumbrous and lacks smoothness.

I prefer the Breithaupt idea: the shoulder muscles gradually lift the forearm until the wrist stands fairly high while the thumb moves towards its destination – the wrist reaches its highest point just before the thumb's new note is due and it is then dropped on to it. All this sounds extremely complicated when described in words, but let Chopin's No. 1 *Étude* (overleaf) illustrate it. The arrows show the gradual up-wards and sideways movement of wrist and forearm, and, in the upward-moving passage, the non-gradual drop on to the thumb terminating the movement. In a downward-moving

55

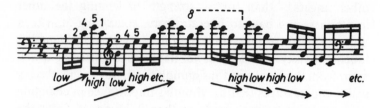

passage – as in the second half of the example – the process is reversed: the highest position of arm and wrist is reached simultaneously with the thumb striking its note, and the hand is then dropped to its next position. Ultimately, when the extent of the arm movement is reduced to a minimum, only a slight up-and-down undulation of the player's arm remains visible.

Scales are treated the same as arpeggios; they are indeed the same thing, with certain notes left out or inserted, respectively.

Finally let me point out that the habit of letting the thumb dangle out of the keyboard when not in action should not be encouraged; the thumb is an invaluable help whether or not taking an active part in the proceedings.

Finger action. The question of the height to which fingers should be raised has – like most technical questions of the kind – no universally valid answer. It depends on the desired musical effect. The player sometimes plays with bent fingers which never (or hardly ever) leave the key, in the so-called 'leggiero' or 'perlé' touch often occurring in Mozart; in heavier passages the fingers are raised but to a moderate height; in octaves the unemployed fingers should not be raised more than is necessary to avoid sounding unwanted keys while the two fingers forming the octave are firmly fixed; in chords all the fingers implicated are fixed and do not leave the key until compelled to do so by the raising of the arm.

Generally speaking the finger, when it is raised, is raised from the knuckle joint, without much movement from the phalanges, which are slightly bent. It is a mistake to hold the knuckles in. Except perhaps in octave playing (and flat-finger 'cantabile' touch) knuckles should be slightly raised, other-wise finger resistance will be impaired – a weakly resistant finger can be overbalanced by arm weight or even by the key. Contact with the key is made through the finger-tips (except in the already mentioned 'cantabile' touch where flat fingers touch the keys with the soft flesh underneath the nail, but this is more properly arm touch than finger touch), and, in order to conserve the strength of the hand-to-finger connec-tion unbroken, it is not advisable to let the nail phalanx make any bending movement in either direction, since it is already, permanently if slightly, bent. This was once con-sidered a very reprehensible habit in the old finger methods, but today we need not be too hard on this type of 'sin'. Generalizations must not be too peremptory as regards the bent finger versus the flat or straight finger practice – both have their advantages in certain situations. Liszt sometimes played with totally straight fingers sloping downwards from a very high wrist; sometimes he held his wrist lower and his fingers bent but hardly visibly raised from the key. Other pianists give the impression of more 'active' finger work, swinging finger movements in a wide radius (sometimes combined with swinging arm movements) and so on, in many variants. Let the musical effect intended, the taste, temperament and ear of the player decide, and, of course, his digital skill and inclination.

Fingering. Closely related to the topic of fingers and finger action is the topic of fingering. Both old and new methods agree on the importance of this.

What finger to put on what key is not a question that greatly agitates the amateur of middling calibre; fumble, hit-or-miss methods are good enough for the sight-reader as long as he produces a reasonable approximation of the music. But the professional pianist, working on a tightrope where deadly danger attends even slight mistakes, cannot afford such risks. His fingering must be carefully thought out, designed to fit his hands, the musical shape and speed of every passage, and, to some extent, even the character of the period the music comes from. If you think this latter observation bizarre, consider the music of Bach where absolute legato may be imperative, without any help from the pedal, by means of 'organist's' fingering, plenty of substitution of fingers and the like – very different from the homophonous pedal-helped ways in which, say, a Chopin nocturne is fingered.

As is well-known, in the early days of the eighteenth century the thumb was not considered a finger at all and was hardly ever used. You need not be quite so conservative as to follow that harpsichord-originated tradition. You need not be afraid to use the thumb, or the little finger for that matter, even on a black key. Apart from the fingering angle, we have discussed the thumb's special character and its place in the general scheme of playing on pp. 54–6.

It is generally accepted today that the practice of scales, arpeggios, chromatic scales etc., imposed on a music student in his early days of study is not done to improve his technique – or only in the limited sense that it teaches him the topography of the keyboard and how to find his way about it almost blindfolded by inculcating certain habits of fingering and positioning. For scales, chromatic and diatonic, and arpeggios (triads or seventh chords) cover, broadly speaking, all the interval material which your hands need to get used to, for secure orientation about the keyboard – and, incidentally, these exercises also cover most of the passage work or figuration which composers use to decorate their piano writing. Such decoration, a characteristic feature of most good piano writing (because slow sustained melody is not in the nature of the instrument, especially when one considers the pre-nineteenth century specimen) – such decorative passage work, then, consists mostly of parts or segments of scales, and arpeggios. It is fairly obvious that those whose keyboard habits, in terms of fingering, were nurtured on early practice of scales and arpeggios, will more readily find the right fingering as well as locate no matter what interval, than those who find the hit-and-miss method less tedious. In some odd way even sight-reading becomes easier by quick and secure displacement of the hand and the instantaneous use of the right fingering – things that are only possible if memory produces immediately what has been stored there from years of practising scales!

The basic fingering of the C major scale (below) serves for nearly all scales, with a few changes where the relative positions of white and black keys make different fingerings

RIGHT   1   2   3   1   2   3   4   5 (1)

LEFT   5   4   3   2   1   3   2   1

more convenient. On this, endless published training manuals give the student all practical information.

It is interesting to note that Liszt recommended (and practised) the use of the C major fingering in all keys, regardless of black-white distinction, as a useful technical exercise. And Chopin, we are told, looked upon the C major scale as the most difficult – because of the divergent shapes of hand and keyboard – and started his pupils off on the scale of B major, as the easiest.

Weight and relaxation

Some of the foregoing discussion may serve as a transition or bridge: we have seen how even in scales and runs, through the agency of the thumb in changing position, the hand and forearm enter into play, either by active movement, or by passively supplying the necessary volume of sound which the fingers – too light and too weak – cannot produce by themselves. It is pretty obvious by now that, broadly speaking, the piano is not played by any one part of the body in isolation but by a compound of all elements functioning in coordination.

Once this is realized you are well into the province of the weight methods: arms, shoulders, even the back and the legs, all legitimate members of the orchestra of the human body, can all be brought to bear, in their different but cohesive ways, on the one complicated instrument, the pianoforte. You do not need a knowledge of anatomy, for it matters little by what technical terms muscles, bones and the like are identified; this side of the problem has received much attention in books about pianoforte technique, and I recommend these books if you are anxious for such detailed knowledge, as I do not intend to deal with it here. Only outlines of what happens in the course of a practical performance can be given here, not a comprehensive theory of pianoforte technique. Theories tend to make rather dry reading, nor can they answer all the questions, except by simplification. They rarely cover the whole truth; on the other hand, certain truths can be bent to fit almost every theory.

It is generally agreed that modern pianoforte technique is based on the idea of relaxation, weight and the economical use of shoulders, arms, hands and fingers, the operative word 'economical' meaning that as little effort as possible should get the greatest possible results, in terms of speed, accuracy and volume.

Perhaps this is the moment to scrutinize the term 'relaxation' because it is sometimes loosely used, and tempts those who want simple answers to see in it a panacea to cure all evils. You already know – and for our purely practical purposes this knowledge is sufficient – that there are sets of muscles to perform certain actions; you must also bear in mind that these muscles are complemented each by another set of muscles whose job it is to perform the opposite kind of action. Stiffness is the result of friction when – as often happens – the wrong set of muscles is involuntarily stimulated to sympathetic action by its counterpart, through some fault of coordination in the nerve centres. If for instance you wish to raise your arm, the opposite set of muscles (the one controlling the downward movement of your arm) may simultaneously come into action, inhibiting or impairing the efficiency of your intended arm movement. You have of course learnt to control such spontaneous intrusion by the non-selected muscles in the course of your daily life; but knowledge, habit and experience all seem to abandon you when you try to play the piano. Those who are gifted in terms of natural physical skill will soon find their own way of using their hands, arms and fingers with the effortless aptitude of animals; others will take a bit longer and require more physiological training, but the problems are not insuperable. What seems fairly obvious is that relaxation is not sufficient – some muscles must be active (and, therefore, unrelaxed) while others rest. You must see to it that your exertion is correctly distributed and not interfered with by detrimental automatisms, and practice is the only way – a short cut is not possible.

Shoulders

The shoulder is the strongest motoric energy centre but it is not required to make too many movements; it can, of course, make such movements as you might wish, up, down, forwards and backwards, but this rarely appears to be necessary in piano playing. Hunching the shoulders (in moments of great emotion) is perhaps too harshly condemned by pedagogues: 'better not' would suit the case more justly, for you should not let emotion convert itself into involuntary movements of any kind. Shoulder movement is used, however, for creating the biggest and, oddly enough, also the smallest volume of sound.

The normal state of the shoulder is one of fixation: it supplies energy which, through the agencies of the upper and forearm, the hand, the finger and the key, is transmitted to the string. It is psychologically important to be aware of the ultimate aim of every act of touch: this aim is the string, not the key. Indeed, as I have already pointed out, it is useful to look upon the key (and the complicated machinery connected to it that we call 'action') as a tool, a continuation of one's finger; this outlook serves to eliminate the key-hitting habit that is so rightly condemned by Matthay. The touch starts at the shoulder (supported, of course, by the rest of the body) and ends at the string; all piano technique is concerned with the right and sensible use of a tool – partly animate, partly inanimate – which impinges upon the string, causing it to make sound.

In this type of technique, movements as such play a less strictly defined part. We may assume that the loosely lying hand, the elastically unimpeded arm and the naturally placed fingers will find their own best, least strenuous way of moving. It is therefore more important to achieve this elasticity and feeling of ease, this internal muscular harmony, than to practise movements. Good and useful though it is to know about 'rotation', 'circling', 'swinging' and the like, there is the danger that most of these can be carried out by stiff arms and hands, entirely satisfactorily to the eye but serving no good purpose. For example, if you bring your arm down on the key with stiff muscles and percussive effect, this will *look* very much the same (although it will sound differently) as the easy, passive and effortless descent of the same arm with liberated weight because of relaxed muscles. You should therefore concentrate not on what the thing looks like but on what it feels like. For the same reason you should make your arm free and let the playing movements look after themselves.

How do you achieve the normal fixed – but not too fixed – state of the shoulder? Some methods recommend lowering the shoulder blades. With the shoulder blades brought fairly close together and pulled slightly downwards you should certainly have a sensation of firmness, and also of a fully used arm-length, of what it means to play 'from the shoulder', instead of just from the elbow as so many young students do. Nevertheless, since it is a good but not an indispensable device, do not turn to it in all situations. By all means try the 'shoulder blades lowering' when more than ordinary endurance is demanded – in powerful octave playing, for instance, or certain Chopin and Liszt studies. But it should not be regarded as a cornerstone of piano technique, nor as a magic wand to dispel any kind of trouble.

This drawing shows the player slightly bent forward, a frequently occurring position

Here the player is shown with lowered shoulder-blades and close-drawn (adduced) arms – a position favoured by the so-called weight methods

Neither of these two positions has universal validity, since movement – flux – is the essence of piano technique

Part Two: Playing the Piano
Arms

Arms can be held close to the body ('adduced') or away from it ('abducted'), they can be fixed in either or both the elbow and wrist joints; they can be selectively relaxed, according to need; they can be rotated around their own axis (forearm rotation) or around an axis laid sideways from the shoulder (upper arm rotation, called *Kreisen* ('circling') by Breithaupt). Rotating the forearm towards the thumb or towards the little finger produces certain anatomical conditions known as 'pronation' and 'supination'. The forearm can make an almost complete turn in one direction – palm pointing upwards – but the upper arm has to be lifted to achieve this in the other direction. In the pronated arm two bones, normally parallel, lay themselves across each other, and this is sometimes found to give a sense of firmness and security to the player.

Busoni apparently favoured the pronated position even for long stretches, with adduced upper arm, 'set' joints and fixed shoulder. In this type of technique you have the sensation of 'carrying your arm in your hand'. Set joints allow you to move with great security, but you may have doubts about delicacy of sound, and greater agility in the smaller joints than in the shoulder. However, by all accounts Busoni's results should dispel such doubts.

But all these things, pronation or supination, adduction or abduction, are static conditions of the arm, held for the length of time required. But during that time your hands and fingers (and your arms, too) move according to the requirements of the music. What about these movements? As I said a little while ago, movements are on the whole not too important from the point of view of early training, and experience confirms that a really relaxed arm and loose-lying hand will instinctively make the right (because the most practical) movement if you only allow them to do so.

Nevertheless, since rotation has already been mentioned, it should be pointed out that the most important 'basic' arm action is that of 'swinging' (for want of a better word). This is

64

an elastic, longitudinal and slightly circular movement of the whole arm, enacted between the shoulder and the finger-tip. All kinds of rotation and circling originate here. Incidentally this is quite a good exercise to achieve the sensation of relaxation, since it goes through all the joints, forcing them to un-stiffen. Forearm rotation is a fragment of this swinging arm movement, and it is almost omnipresent in all piano playing, usually in conjunction with finger action. In a figure like that shown below a very slight rotation towards the little finger will take place regardless of whether the fingers are raised or not.

For the left hand read an inversion of this

Trill and vibrato

In a trill (which cannot be satisfactorily done by fingers alone) the rotation component is quite noticeable. Difficulty in playing trills is often caused by insufficient coordination of the vibrato and the rotation components. The term 'vibrato' describes fine trembling movements with which a smaller part of the anatomy subdivides, as it were, the initial impetus given to it by a bigger one. To understand this think of what happens when you knock two or three times on a door: the initial impetus (which may come from the shoulder or the upper arm) supplies the energy for a 'burst' of small movements carried out by the forearm, the wrist or even the fingers (this is relevant to the trill). Depending on the strength of the impetus, these quick trembling movements will last a shorter or longer time, and when the impetus is exhausted, it can be renewed by another movement from the shoulder – or from wherever it came originally. Quick repeated notes, like the octaves in Schubert's *Erlking* or in Liszt's *Hungarian Rhapsody No. 6*, depend for their efficiency on the vibrato technique just described. The vibrato, which is also present in rapid octave playing, repeated chords, long staccato passages, etc., is one of the most important weapons in the pianist's armoury, second perhaps only to the forearm rotation. To avoid fatigue in long repeated-octave passages some pianists use the device of 'in-and-out' (stretching out and pulling in the arm at regular intervals while vibrating it) or 'up-and-down' undulation of the wrist-plus-forearm, both of which are useful for renewing the original impetus, or rather for making it last longer.

The trill, then, is a combination of forearm rotation and finger vibrato. Rotation will be more in evidence in forte and fortissimo trills, finger motion in the lower dynamic grades. Some teachers recommend the following exercise to get over the stubborn problem of a sluggish, inhibited trill: rest a finger – say the thumb – on a key, then raise the other finger concerned in the execution of the trill and bring it repeatedly and with the greatest possible speed on the neighbouring key, by means of finger vibrato. Repeat this with the other finger held static and your thumb vibrating. Finally allow both your fingers to vibrate and the arm to rotate, all at the same time. A good natural trill on the piano has something in common with that on a string instrument where the guiding principle is that one finger is kept static on the string which the other finger vibrates up and down; a pianoforte trill is not quite the same because both fingers have to move, but it is similar in that one finger moves less than the other.

Conclusions

I can now sum up the few aspects of pianoforte technique that I have touched upon here.

Technique is the ability, gained by experience and practice, to bring the anatomy of the human body to bear on the instrument, and in so doing to achieve the best possible results with the least possible exertion.

It is not imperative but useful for you to know something about the inside of the instrument, nor is it absolutely necessary for you to be familiar with the laws of anatomy

66

except in the way of purely practical application.

You must create in your body a state of muscular harmony (sometimes mis-named 'relaxation') in which alternative possibilities of tensing and relaxing groups of muscles are properly coordinated and controlled by will.

The shoulder, as the strongest energy centre, should receive special attention. It is not very mobile, but it is capable of producing both the biggest and the smallest volume of sound. Impetus for all kinds of arm movement comes from the shoulder, of which rotation and vibrato are the most frequently used.

Volume depends on weight, or sometimes (not often) pressure. Transmission of weight (or pressure) originates in the shoulder and is aimed at the string, not the key. The transmission itself is an act of leverage – not of brute force – and therefore you should feel most muscular exertion as an upward action, against the shoulder. Keys should not be hit or squeezed.

All acts are compound ones, involving everything from the shoulder downwards, and it is useless to try and isolate any particular part of your body – for example the fingers – and make it work alone.

It is safe to assume that once the muscular harmony (or relaxation) is achieved and is present in your mind, your body will automatically find the right – that is the most practical and economical – movements. It follows that teachers should perhaps be less preoccupied with movements as such than with creating the conditions necessary to produce them.

Unless absolutely necessary you should not use forearm pressure to get more volume because it is nonproductive and detrimental, and will exhaust you in a very short time. Pressure from the shoulder is unavoidable in big chord playing, but you should stop using it this side of the fatigue border. *All muscular exertion should remain this side of fatigue.* Normal muscular commitment, which is all that you need for piano playing, is not felt at all.

Since all pianists need to acquire the habit of easy acclimatization to unfamiliar instruments it must be stressed that your finger-tips will cease to transmit messages about key-resistance to your brain if your arm is tense.

Ultimately you should lose all consciousness of technique. Hard work and practice help you reach this ideal, and then technique ceases to exist and Art takes over – Art which is concerned with the higher things of the mind and the soul, amongst which it ranges freely and easily.

Seven
On Pedalling, Considered as a Fine Art*
*With apologies to Mr Thomas de Quincey

Anton Rubinstein called the pedal the soul of the piano, and Liszt said that without it the pianoforte would be just some kind of 'hackbrett'. It is remarkable that despite its recognized importance this element of piano playing has been practically ignored by music teachers except for some vague though well-meant advice against 'over-pedalling'. Even intelligent pianists often limit their comments on the pedal to an indulgent and humorous admission that it can hide a multitude of sins. What sins we are not told.

The 'loud' pedal

The action of the pedal on the ingenious mechanical contraption of the damper has been described in Chapter 3, but a brief summary will be helpful here. In a modern piano the strings can continue to vibrate and sound for quite some time after the key and hammer actions have terminated. Obviously this would result in an intolerable confusion of sound, and the damper, resting upon the upper sides of the strings while the hammers strike them from below, silences the sound when the key is released. But when you depress the right pedal the damper is lifted off the strings, thus returning to them all or part of their natural sound duration.

If you understand this you will also understand why the classics used the expressions 'con sordino' and 'senza sordino' to mean, respectively, 'without' and 'with' pedal, and not the reverse. The classical usage is much more in keeping with the real facts, not immediately discernible by the eye, than our 'Ped . . . . . .*' marking, which is in keeping only with the *visual* fact of the pedal's down-and-up movement corresponding with the up-and-down movement of the damper action – perhaps an eloquent comment on the superficiality of our spoon-fed generation, wanting to know only what to do with hands and feet to get such results as may be desired, but not the reason why. Some modern composers have adopted the more accurate notation ⌞   ⌟ indicating the exact points at which your foot should operate and release the pedal. When continuously changing pedalling is wanted something like the sign ⌞⋀⋀⋀⌟ is used, or even ⌞∿∿∿∿∿ for the pedal 'trill' or pedal 'vibrato'. Some composers (Bartók among them) indicate '$\frac{1}{2}$ Ped' but leave any smaller divisions to the player's discretion.

The mention of half pedal and the like reminds me that I have already let the cat out of the bag. What I wish to write about is, of course, firstly, the various possible timings of pedal depression and, secondly, the idea that the depth of that depression is also capable of variation. But before such analytical treatment of the matter is possible, let us examine the broad question of what Anton Rubinstein, Franz Liszt and countless others meant by calling the pedal the soul of the piano. Were these great men just fantasists, maintaining that the crazy visions of their imaginations were the sober truth? Or is it rather the case that truth – not, admittedly, the sober truth – touched with crazy imagination becomes Art?

The pedal as the soul of the piano

How it is that the great pianist, the inspired artist on the concert platform, beguiles and bewitches his hearers into believing in the beauty of his particular sound, so unlike any other sound produced by someone less inspired, on the same instrument, in the same concert hall, before the same audience? It cannot all be make-believe, mass hypnosis, self-delusion on the part of the listeners – some of whom are possibly good and serious musicians. Certainly there is a mystery, a magical element, part inspiration, part hypnotic personality in contact with higher things, which it transmits (like a medium in a trance) – things like that defy analysis. Every artist who *is* an artist has experienced the mystery that sometimes makes a performance more than a performance, and it would be foolish to deny that such mystery and such magic do exist, even if we assume them to be figments of the consciousness or of the imagination. There are, however, elements that *can* be analysed, since the artist, even in his trance, does deal with the easily defined tools of his craft, with fingers, wrists, arms, keys and – last but not least – the pedals.

I am quite convinced that the proper use of the sustaining pedal constitutes about half, if not more, of what we call 'tone', and that the individual ways of using it differ so much between artists as to account for some of the baffling enigma why the sound produced by one artist is so different from that produced by another, even when their skills and instrument are the same.

No doubt there are other things to be considered: phrasing, which has far more to do with 'tone' than we are aware, balance as between component elements of chords, idiosyncrasies of fingering, the relative strength of right and left hand, and much else. But let us, for a few moments, consider the 'soul of the piano' – the pedal.

Timing

One uses the pedal in three ways: simultaneously with the sound, after the sound (syncopated pedal, the most common method), or before the sound (anticipated pedal).

This third way – the anticipated pedal – is relatively rare but not as rare as one might think. Many pianists put the pedal down before they start playing, partly to avoid too much 'attack' in the first sound, by mobilizing, as it were, the auxiliaries (= harmonics) even before the 'regulars' move into action. As an example, in Beethoven's Concerto in G Major the opening G major chord of the solo pianoforte gains a more ethereal quality if the pedal slightly anticipates the hands. I do not deny that some of this may be psychological but if so the action is still fully justified. The actual lapse of time between lifting the damper and playing your first note, or notes, is unimportant. It can be a split second, or a minute, just as you wish.

But in syncopated pedalling the lapse of time becomes very important. Obviously, the longer the time that elapses between key-depression and pedal-depression, the clearer will be the resulting sound effect; if this vital time-lapse is cut short there is a risk that remnants of previous sounds, harmonically unrelated, will be perpetuated by the pedal, thus creating a most disagreeable mixture. Sometimes the fault is not too noticeable in a small room, but the concert hall, with its much higher reverberation component, shows up premature use of the sustaining pedal with surprising brutality. Strictures on pianists' 'over-pedalling' should in many cases be directed at 'pedalling too soon' or 'not enough change of pedal', but one cannot expect listeners or critics to diagnose exactly what causes a sometimes intolerable confusion of sound in which all finer points of harmonic progressions, modulations as well as the melodic line, become a total loss.

The rule 'play first, pedal afterwards' is of permanent and universal validity, but, like all rules, it has its exceptions. Simultaneous pedalling is indeed more correctly regarded by musicians as the exception to the rule.

What are the situations, then, where simultaneous pedalling becomes the rule and not the exception? One example is:

Composers often use this kind of notation, instead of clearly indicating the correct sound because it is taken for granted

that any self-respecting pianist will use the pedal to prolong the bass note A natural without which the chord would be incomplete (unless, of course, a $^6_4$ chord is intended). In this example the hand must relinquish the note A natural at the very moment

it is sounded, and move on with the greatest possible speed –
an action known as a 'leap' – to the other four notes of the
chord, leaving the necessary continuance of the bass note to
the pedal. It follows from this that unless the pedal acts simultaneously with the beginning of sound, thus catching the note
the player wishes to be caught – as in a net – the chord
will be there but without its vitally important component,
the bass. This is a frequent fault, and not only among pupils.
Insufficient theoretical grounding, an ear that is not
trained to hear primarily harmonic functions, or the functions of individual notes within chords (which is more
important than recognizing their pitch), an insufficient curiosity, a mental laziness inhibiting any wish to read between the
notes or to correct any slip the composer may have made in
his notation, just because the necessary adjustment is 'not in
the score' – these are some of the reasons why a performance may fail to be worthy of the name of 'interpretation'.
For playing all the notes correctly is *not* an interpretation,
and the right way of using the pedal is practically never in the
score.

The time-honoured professorial joke that the best way of
using the pedal is not to use it must be resisted with all
possible vigour. Not using the pedal is a barbarity, committed
in the name of some sort of 'truth'. But X-ray photographs are
not art, even if what they show is part of the truth. (I am
bound to admit exceptions to this, too. Special effects demand
special measures; but these special cases are few and far
between.)

Another case when simultaneous pedal must be used is
when a very short but yet living sound is required, a kind of
plucked, pizzicato effect, as for example in Liszt's *Vallée
d'Obermann*. The action of the pedal must begin exactly with

the sound and cease exactly, or almost exactly, when the hand leaves the key, no matter how quickly. There will be no noticeable after-sound, but the effect will be somewhat similar to that made by a string player plucking his strings with his right hand while the left continues to vibrate.

Again in the opening bar of Liszt's Sonata in B Minor I prefer this 'pizzicato ma vibrato' to the completely dry staccato favoured by some pianists; and especially at the very end of that great work there is, for me, a test note – the player who, instead of letting that last deep B natural boom and reverberate for a while, makes it sound like a short dry slap stands convicted as an unfeeling vandal. Pedal, then, can be simultaneous in two senses: that of *beginning* with the manual action and that of *ceasing* with the ending of the manual action – these do not necessarily go together. I frequently adopt the practice of taking my hands off at once, the pedal only a little later. The opposite process – pedal coming off first, then the hand – occurs very rarely in practice, but should not be totally ruled out theoretically. In fact certain 'flageolet' effects, much favoured by twentieth-century composers, have just that process as their basic factor.

The following example comes from my own personal store of effects (I do not force it on pupils!). The chord will sound

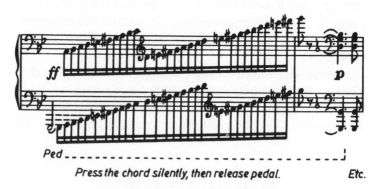

Press the chord silently, then release pedal.   Etc.

like very soft organ register, without attack. It is true that the rests are, in this case, sacrificed.

Pedal vibrato

An important device, much practised by pianists of our time, is the pedal vibrato, or pedal trill. The idea is to use the pedal even for rapid scale passages but to ensure that it will not obscure the pronunciation of the notes. In Beethoven (and after) one finds passages marked forte or fortissimo which, taken without pedal, would sound hard and dry, with the pedal sustained throughout intolerably confused, with intermittent pedal, uneven; in such cases the vibrato pedal is recommended, provided it is skilfully applied. Skilful indeed must be the player who synchronizes his pedalling with his fingers so perfectly that every note of a scale is individually pedalled! The most one can hope for is a good approximation, and only at moderate speed. For pre-Beethoven music (Mozart, for instance) the vibrato pedal is not recommended.

(Perhaps this is the place to affirm that, contrary to a once fashionable belief leading to malpractice, Mozart was no harpsichord composer, and that the instrument he played and wrote for had all the appurtenances, if not the size and sonority, of the modern pianoforte – including the pedal. Readers will have found more reference to this in Chapter 3.)

The use of the pedal

It is with Beethoven that the pedal takes on an enormously enlarged part in music for the piano. For not only was he the first composer to mark pedalling in many places of his piano sonatas and concerti (Mozart only did so sporadically), but it is evident that, with Beethoven, for the first time in the history of the piano, pedalling becomes an integral part of the intended sound effect, and thus an integral part of the composition. Two examples can be quoted to illustrate this: the opening of the rondo movement from the 'Waldstein' Sonata (Op. 53) (overleaf), and the famous recitative from the Sonata in D minor (Op. 31 No. 2) (overleaf). In both these examples – and there are many others – Beethoven deliberately disregards changes of harmony; but then

Beethoven always made his own rules. Nor is there much strength in the argument that deafness was the cause of the odd pedal markings because in the early works – written in Beethoven's twenties, long before deafness set in – there are similar oddities to be found.

At this point we should consider, if briefly, the advisability or otherwise of using pedals in Bach's keyboard music. There are passionate arguments on either side and most of them carry a grain of conviction. A good case can be made out against performing Bach on the pianoforte at all (for he did not compose for that instrument, nor indeed did he like the sound of it), but in accepting this point of view one would deprive oneself and countless music lovers of some of the greatest music ever written, which would be a pity. Perhaps the truth is that Bach's music is abstract and can be divorced from the medium originally intended, as can be seen from his own arrangements of his works; and that, once the music is transferred to, and performed on, the pianoforte, it is the right of the player, so long as he is endowed with taste and sense of style, to use all the resources of his instrument. Trying to imitate the sound of a harpsichord on the pianoforte, by using no pedal, is a totally negative, inartistic and unsuccessful proceeding.

The 'soft' and sostenuto pedals

Time was when American piano makers disgusted serious
music lovers by enriching the piano with additional mechanisms regulated by pedals – mechanisms which imitated the
sound of drums, cymbals, wind machines and the like.
Luckily these innovations met their deserved fate and are no
longer remembered. Much more serious and likely to survive
are the so-called 'soft' pedal (or 'una corda' pedal), and the
sostenuto pedal, an invention of Messrs. Steinway & Sons,
but, now that their patent has expired, fairly generally used
by other makers.

The terms 'una corda' and 'soft 'pedal are in fact misnomers
because the shifting mechanism makes the hammer touch
two instead of three strings, but never just one, and because
it does not make the tone appreciably softer, only somewhat
muted, or in some instruments slightly nasal. Composers
since Beethoven, notably Chopin and Liszt, followed the
Master in marking 'una corda', but there is a valid objection
that the decision to use the soft pedal should be left to the
player – since the effect varies so much from instrument to
instrument, and since the inclination to use it also varies
according to the habits and temperament of individual
players. In any case you should not resort to the soft pedal
every time you wish to play softly, for you have other,
non-mechanical, means to achieve that end.

The 'sostenuto' pedal, described in Chapter 3, is a very
useful device, which sustains any individual notes or chords
you may wish to prolong without affecting the rest of the
texture (such as a 'pedal' bass remaining constant, with
shifting harmonies above it). Certain organ-like effects in
Busoni's Bach transcriptions are impossible without this
'middle pedal'. I recommend working this pedal with the left
foot.

The 'una corda' pedal is used slightly in advance of the
sound, but the sostenuto pedal must always be depressed
after the sound, and always by itself (never in conjunction
with the 'loud pedal').

Part Two: Playing the Piano

Finally, a piece of advice to the untrained: keep your heel on the ground when using a pedal. The pedal itself is moved by the tip of your toe, and you can vary the depth to which the pedal is depressed. Kicking the pedal or beating time with the left foot are not signs of a fiery temperament, but abominably bad habits to be abolished at nursery stage.

All this, and a few complementary things attempted in the next chapter, is Pedalling considered as a Fine Art.

Have we laid bare the soul of the piano? Have we caught the 'moonlight streaming down on a landscape' (Busoni)? I hardly think so. But at least one minuscule element of the great mystery that gave rise to this chapter has been brought nearer the imaginary microscope which could, in time, examine it.

Eight

Two 'Fallacies':
Singing Tone and Legato

The complex of problems that surround pedalling, discussed in the previous chapter, raises the further problems: does singing tone really exist on the piano? and does legato really exist? Scientists are certain that they do not, but let us for a few moments ignore them and assume that they could be wrong.

That there is a fundamental and ever-present connection between pedalling and our two 'fallacies' cannot be doubted, and this connection has been explored in the foregoing chapter.

There are many subtle and significant ways in which the pedals, by mobilizing all or some of the harmonics, or by stimulating the sympathetic vibrations of non-active strings, can influence tone quality. But the extent of such stimulation is not always at the player's command and disposal, and can hardly be formulated for practical use. Who can make accurate calculations as to the split-second timing of each pedal depression or its depth or the exact moment of its termination? Obviously, these things must be left to the player's instinct, and in this, as in other respects, different personalities will do differently. Nor will every instrument demand the same treatment or react to it in the same way. (This point has been briefly touched upon in Chapter 6.) Here we come upon one of the secret reasons why each individual produces a different sound from the same instrument: some players have the gift of instant assimilation and can sense any peculiarities of an instrument and feel at home on it almost at once; but others may find this completely impossible or else need a long time to warm up. And yet since we cannot follow the example of our happier fiddling colleagues and carry our bulky instrument about we should be able to feel at ease at once on any reasonably good instrument. This obviously relevant aspect of our technique has not received much attention from pedagogues. It is generally assumed to be a question of relaxation. If certain muscles are not sufficiently trained to obey the command 'remain inactive' the resulting stiffness in shoulder, arm or hand affects the sensibility of the fingertips and impedes them in their task of feeling the resistance of the key – a resistance which, as is well-known, varies from instrument to instrument.

Sir James Jeans once uttered a now celebrated dictum that it made no difference whether a piano key was hit by a finger, a fist or an umbrella handle. But he did not take into account one concrete factor, the pedal, and one partly abstract factor, the player's physical condition as determined by some very illusive happenings in his mind.

It is indeed possible to make an ugly harsh noise – no one will deny that. That it is also possible to create beautiful sound (within the limitation of each instrument), and that there are differences of touch – not merely those of loud and soft – is a matter of practical experience which everyone who has ears to hear will be aware of, no matter how difficult or impossible it might be to prove it scientifically.

Let us, in fairness to Sir James, admit that this umbrella-handle theory claims validity only for *the single note*. But it cannot be doubted that the piano (not an instrument specially invented for the purpose of hitting a single note louder or softer) offers a great deal of variety when several notes are sounded, together or one after the other.

Anyone can try this out by playing a common chord, spread over, say, two octaves and a half. If you first

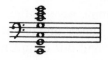

stress the highest note in the chord (the natural thing to do) you get a certain sound quality, something that is known as 'colour'. Under the fingers of a Rachmaninov type pianist this note could resemble the sound of a trumpet. Now try to stress another of the components constituting the chord, the alto or one of the lower notes, or even the bass itself, and observe how the character of the sound changes. (This is, incidentally, quite a good exercise for the fingers.)

Phrasing, surprisingly perhaps, but undoubtedly, is one factor amongst many which go to make up 'singing tone'. The sound of a chord depends on the dynamic balance, or the relation of the constituents one to another. Similarly the sound of a melodic line depends on the disposition of the slight voluntary irregularities with which a player gives every phrase expression and eloquence. Nothing could be more wrong than to insist on evenness. Our ears are so conditioned by hearing melodies performed with slight crescendi and diminuendi that the absence of such shades of expression would make them unbearably dull. The listener would have the impression of hearing single disconnected notes, reluctant to shape themselves into phrases, merely living a mechanical, metronomic life. This is one of the greatest enemies of the living phrase, and of that elusive property in some odd way connected with it, the singing tone.

Needless to say, these shades really must be shades – hardly noticeable inflexions, discernible only to the finest ear strained to its utmost. If kept at this level such slight inflexions will not prevent, but rather contribute to, that impression of evenness in the melodic line which is a basic need of the musical listener. Let us remember that strings, wind, the human voice – all can, and do, make crescendo and diminuendo even within the same note. The piano can only do diminuendo – but it can still make a living, growing organism out of a phrase by means of well placed and musically felt variations of sound.

No doubt the singing tone on the piano is partly an illusion; but to do everything in his power to create such an illusion is surely one of the foremost tasks of the great illusionist that the great pianist has to be.

It is easy to see that the element of illusion also plays an important part in what we call legato. Obviously the *perfect* legato – the perfectly connected notes of a slow-moving melody, of which other instruments and the human voice are capable – is not within the power of the piano. Busoni, whose authority cannot be doubted, admonished students of the pianoforte not to chase after the unattainable ideal of legato; and one of the salient principles of Matthay's method was the theory that the act of touch is always staccato. Perhaps this needs an explanation, for those who have not read Matthay, or experienced his teaching.

This theory, then, assumes the existence of a permanent state, that of resting, of the player's arms and hands in relation to the keyboard; against this background of resting, the limb concerned in the actual 'act of touch' carries out short-lived efforts (Matthay calls this 'the added impetus') to create the requisite sound. Since such effort, according to Matthay, must cease the very moment sound begins to be heard, it follows that only staccato exists, the effects of staccato or legato depending on the level of 'resting' which, in staccato playing, is on the surface of the key, in legato playing nearer the key bed, or on it if necessary. (A quotation from Matthay has already been given in Chapter 3.)

One may doubt if this theory still holds today. The isolation of active fingers from passive arm is perhaps a little too cut-and-dried (one likes to think of every act on the keyboard as a combined operation in which everything takes part), and it is doubtful whether the 'lighter' resting of the arm, because some of its weight must be carried by the shoulder muscles, can still be properly called 'resting'. But, be that as it may, the interesting idea that a legato effect can be achieved by a staccato action (but not *vice versa*) still assumes that it is possible to play legato on the piano.

A single attempt at listening to a recording tape played backwards very slowly will convince the scientist at any rate that it is not possible. Every note will begin with a crescendo, the reverse of the diminuendo which actually happens to the note when the tape is played normally.

Thanks to piano makers, however, and their unceasing efforts to improve strings, sound-board and damper, the prolongation of sound after the note is struck is today not a very grave problem, given a player with an adequate technique and, even more important, the gift of creating illusion. The diminuendo that follows the initial sound on the modern piano is so slight that the naked ear can hardly perceive it; and the average listener (who is not a scientist) is so conditioned through years of listening to piano playing, good, bad, and indifferent, that he hears what he wishes to hear: perfect legato.

A judge, attempting to sum up on the evidence presented here, would presumably say something like the following:

A case has been made out that such things as singing tone and legato (both helped by pedal) do in actual fact exist in piano playing, and should not, therefore, be dismissed as fictitious or fallacious, albeit their existence is difficult to prove rationally. One may argue from the negative to the positive: bad, ugly tone undeniably exists, and many players have no legato; therefore the positive opposite, namely beautiful tone and good legato, also exist; but this may be sophistry. It is admitted that much of the artistic objective in this case is achieved by imponderable things: imagination, make-believe, black magic or hypnotism, all of which are generically called 'illusion'. Illusion in Art is not a crime (albeit cheating is involved) but a proper prerogative of the artist, and the extent to which he succeeds in creating it should be one of the standards whereby his artistic stature is measured.

Nine
Intermezzo One: On Teachers and Teaching

Before we continue our investigations let us pause for a moment to pay tribute to some great but modest men, who have, in the past, fashioned generation after generation of instrumentalists – the great teachers of the piano.

Some were great pianists, like Chopin and Liszt, who coming from the age of universality – before the musical profession split into groups of specialists – took a pride in being all things to all men: composer, pianist, conductor, teacher, it was all expected of them. If Chopin (who did not conduct, and who virtually limited his composing to the one medium of the piano) did not live up to this requirement, the reason was undoubtedly his fragile health, and consequent short expectation of life. I will deal with the two greatest figures of the pianoforte's Golden Age, Chopin and Liszt, at some greater depth in Part Three. This diversion is intended to underline their importance as teachers.

Chopin was undoubtedly very interested in teaching, and his ideas on technique – influenced though they were by his own somewhat old-fashioned early training – departed boldly on the road to discovery, especially in the matter of fingering. He made notes, we are told, containing ideas for a projected book on a new method, but, alas, died before the book could be written, and most of the notes were destroyed. One imagines that his ideas on fingering might have been revolutionary, and he was keen to make practising intelligent and interesting for the pupil, and not a soul-killing waste of time. Unfortunately none of his pupils (not even Carl Mikuli) became famous enough to carry the torch of the Chopin method to future generations.

Liszt, luckier in his choice of pupils than Chopin (possibly because his world fame attracted the very cream of pianistic youth anxious to learn some of the magician's secrets) was himself the pupil of Carl Czerny in early childhood – a man of conservative views and rigid pedantry. More of him also in Part Three; sufficiently relevant to our subject, however, is the fact that Liszt soon grew out of this old-fashioned 'fingers-only' school (in which the pupil was encouraged to dispel the boredom of practising scales and exercises by reading books at the same time!). And yet he never attempted to pass on his own entirely new technique to his pupils – except by frequently performing in front of them, thus allowing those who had ears to hear and eyes to see to follow in their master's footsteps. And this they did, some very skilfully, becoming famous in their turn. In teaching by example rather than by explanation (not to mention his human greatness and ever-helpful generosity) Liszt was, by common consent, one of the greatest teachers who ever lived.

It was during Liszt's lifetime that an unknown German musician named Ludwig Deppe started teaching a new method based on arm weight, relaxation, hand position and the like. It was a revolution the effects of which are felt today – fortunately the effects were beneficial. Deppe himself had no very successful pupils. His American pupil Amy Fay, who admired him deeply, achieved fame for herself and her teacher only by her charming book *Music Study in Germany*. Deppe made the first step towards transforming pianoforte teaching from untidy, empirical, trial-and-error experimentalism into a scientific system, based on more or less accurately observed natural laws. From then on artists and teachers were for ever divided into separate groups – perhaps not altogether a good thing.

The rest of the story is well-known. Great and influential teachers came into the world of piano playing: Tobias Matthay in England, R. M. Breithaupt in Germany, Robert Teichmueller in Austria, Felix Blumenfeld in Russia, Isidore Phillipe and Marguerite Long in France, Sándor Kovács in Hungary – all estimable people who did great service to pianism by systematizing the growing mass of new ideas first introduced by Ludwig Deppe.

There are slight national differences within the basic similarities: for instance in French methods there is an 'accent' on fingers, both literally and metaphorically. But the only lone wolf in this assembly of 'methodists' (if you will forgive the joke) was Leschetizky, a very great teacher who loudly proclaimed that he had no method at all; and his pupils, amongst whom figure such exalted names as Paderewski, Gabrilowitsch, Ignaz Friedmann, Benno Moiseiwitch, Mark Hamburg, Artur Schnabel, Frank Merrick and many others, tend to confirm their master's disclaimer of a method.

If I may be permitted to make a general observation on teaching: no teacher can put anything into a pupil which is not already there. He can only awake what is lying dormant, and guide it towards possible short cuts, tending and nurturing it as it grows. In a manner of speaking, teaching anybody anything is really impossible. In the process of doing the impossible it is undeniably the teacher who learns more than the pupil, and this, in my humble opinion, is the ultimate value of teaching.

Ten
Intermezzo Two: On Practising

Pianists can be divided into the following three categories: those who practise a lot and admit it; those who practise a lot but deny it; and those who do not practise and, therefore, are no pianists.

There are very few amongst us, perhaps one born in each century, on whom the fairies bestow the gift of doing miracles without work. Nor is such a fairy necessarily a good fairy, or such a cradle a happy one. For inherited genius, like inherited fortune, must be used, turned, invested, not simply lived on. Beware of the elderly grasshopper, for his riches may run out before his life is finished; in our profession, the ant has it every time.

Practising is not just a daily formality of passing a few hours in consolidating or improving your technique. Indeed the higher you climb on the way to the summit, the more rarefied the air and the more difficult the progress; the idea that only students need to practise and not mature artists is a complete fallacy. When you assume that your technique is fully adequate because you can scamper about the keyboard with amazing celerity – have you asked yourself if you have devoted sufficient time to coming to grips with the great intellectual problems of music? It does not follow that, because you have learnt to play all Chopin's studies impressively, you can make light of Beethoven's *'Hammerclavier'* fugue.

You should regard practising as a physical and mental training; it continues for your lifetime (professional lifetime, that is) and demands the fully committed resources of both body and mind.

Memory must be trained, be it never so strong, to cope with greater complexities as your repertoire fills up; and when it is full to capacity your mind will make its selection of what to forget in order to admit something new – rather as a sponge wipes a place free on a full blackboard. This may sound too subtle to be included amongst the things denoted by that unsubtle word 'practising', and yet this is where it belongs.

Practising helps memory – and memory helps practising. You could argue that memory does not matter and should not be one of the yardsticks whereby artists are measured. After all before Liszt every artist had the score before him in public performance, and today's demands in this respect are just a silly prejudice. True; but your competitors are ready to bow to the popular prejudice, and if you wish to take part in the competition you must accept its terms without cavilling. Besides it is really true that you will play better, and more freely and vividly from memory than when you are impeded by looking at the hypnotic page (unless of course anxiety paralyses your faculties).

It is useful, indeed advisable, to start memorizing any new work (new, that is, to you) away from the instrument. You read the score, and analyse it formally, harmonically and technically – all without using the piano. This kind of memorizing should include even motoric aspects of the piece, like movements of the arms and choice of touch and fingering, all worked out in your imagination before any sound is made. Then you should go to the piano and play the whole piece (or as much of it as possible) from memory, not using the copy. At this point changes will occur as your fingers improve on the preliminary designs worked out in the abstract. The next stage is a play-through, in imagination only, without piano, without music. It is immaterial what else you do simultaneously; you can go for a walk or sit in an armchair. The final stage is the performance, full-dress, by heart. By this time the process of learning should be complete; if it is not, repeat the whole process. In this way the visual memory is exercised and developed first, and the motoric and aural ones subsequently.

I believe the famous pianist and teacher Josef Hofmann recommended something rather similar to students.

Above all steep yourself in the music until you are certain that you understand it. By 'understanding' I mean an ability to follow the workings of the composer's mind in the technical sense: harmony must be an open book to you (by early training); even the smallest passing note or suspension deserves special attention – this is even more important, because less stereotyped, than form. Furthermore every musician should teach himself to read an orchestral score (including C clefs and transposing instruments) unless his college has looked after his education in that respect. For it is impossible to understand and very difficult to learn a concerto part if attention is not paid to what the orchestra is doing.

Of course, there should be, in a day of comprehensive practising, enough time for purely technical exercise. No matter how efficient your technique, there is always something that can be improved, a problem not yet solved, a weakness you wish to eliminate. If you are aware of a chronic defect (such as a weak trill or unsatisfactory octaves), it is best to invent your own exercise to combat the weakness. If you are not inventive, use relevant parts of Chopin or Liszt studies or episodes from the classics. If your rhythm is strong you may risk the method of rhythmic variations (varying rhythmic patterns) used by some pianists.

Do not allow artistic imagination and technique to get too widely separated one from the other; they do belong together. It is a mistake to think that practising 'without expression' (!) or 'without pedal' will get you anywhere, or that bashing the piano very loudly, regardless of musical considerations, will be useful. By all means practise fast pieces slowly, if you must, but for God's sake, and for music's sake, do not practise slow movements prestissimo.

Watch your breathing – it should be regular and through the diaphragm. You can pay attention to this while you are practising, but later, in performance, it must be automatic.

Whatever you do, test the efficacy of your method immediately by playing through what you have practised. Progress must be made daily.

A good principle I impart to pupils: there is no such thing as a Difficult Piece. A piece is either impossible – or it is easy.

The process whereby it migrates from one category to the other is known as practising.

Eleven
The Piano Combined with Other Instruments

Chamber music

There is a popular fallacy that the pianist who fails to make his mark as a soloist should become an accompanist or chamber music player. This is totally untrue. The player who is equal to the piano part of Schubert's *Erlking* or that of Dvorák's Piano Quintet must be a virtuoso of the first order; and it is only fair to state that not all virtuosi of the first order possess the sensitivity of the great chamber musician, even if their technique is adequate.

Another fallacy, held even by some good musicians, is that the piano, when married to one or several other instruments (since chamber music can be a polygamous art), must at all times behave in a modestly subdued manner, providing gentle background for the livelier rest of the ensemble, otherwise the cry goes up 'too loud'. But if you look into old scores, printed at the time of the great Viennese classics, you will be astonished to find that Mozart and Beethoven often composed sonatas 'for pianoforte with violin accompaniment'. Granted this may have been lip service to tradition, but the very existence of such a tradition proves that the piano was by no means the poor companion shadowing the brilliantly leading violin, but rather the other way about. This was the classical view, and it gives us a valuable hint as to how the piano should be treated by the intelligent chamber musician: not as a slave, nor as a master, but *primus inter pares*.

Mozart was theoretically still rooted in the 'violin accompaniment' idea, but nevertheless gave the violin the lead occasionally, usually in the slow movements. His marvellous, unfailing instinct for the true nature of the instruments employed told him that the violin could sing and should not therefore accompany all the time, but that the piano had a greater mobility and comprehensive range more suited to figuration, arabesque and embellishment than to sustained melody. But Mozart was a practical musician, not a theorist. If he sometimes made the violin fill in with double stops or chords while the pianist enjoyed magical moments of melodic expansion, this was not necessarily a concession to the contemporary sound-idea which favoured the piano, but possibly a wise precaution on his part. For he was well aware that violin playing at the time was of a lower technical standard than piano playing – father Leopold notwithstanding – and that most of his tunes were safest in the hands of a pianist, preferably his own.

Most of this also applies to Beethoven's sonatas 'for pianoforte with violin accompaniment' (a misleading description which I believe he dropped in favour of 'Sonata for violin and pianoforte'). Here the piano gets an even bigger share than in Mozart, and the pianist has passage work of great rapidity, vigorous octaves and other things in no way easier than what is required of the soloist in a concerto. It is evident that the pianist who 'effaces' himself in these works does not do justice to the music. But it is evident, too, that a compromise is necessary to reach a tolerable balance. The pianist should play his part then with precision and brilliance when the situation allows it but without drowning his partner, and only rarely become the modest accompanist. Remember that the piano can be the perfect foil, but its volume, especially when the use of pedal is unrestricted, can also prove fatal for the single string instrument – particularly the violoncello. Beethoven wrote five 'cello sonatas, but without ever succeeding in solving the balance problem. This, then, has to be the problem of the interpreter, who can solve it by being careful and circumspect.

It is evident that chamber music is essentially the art of compromise. Liszt, who hated all compromise, called it contemptuously '*Jammermusik*' (a German pun, too tedious to explain), but Brahms, with compromise in his blood, wrote some of his best music in this form: sonatas for violin, 'cello, horn, clarinet (all with piano), trios, quartets, even a quintet where a single piano happily holds the balance to a whole string quartet. Dvořák, whose interest in the piano as a solo instrument (apart from an early, not very distinguished concerto, and some short pieces) was almost non-existent, followed Brahms in composing almost exactly the same number of works for piano trio, quartet and quintet, in which a native instinct for sound and clarity of texture greatly improves on some of Brahms's impenetrable thickness of writing. Mozart and Beethoven gave the piano undisputed star parts in their trios and quartets. And Haydn's piano trios are all but 'piano solo' – the violin and 'cello parts being mostly negligible doublings of the pianist's right and left hands. This is hardly chamber music in our sense of the word; but the great charm of the material used justifies some 'editing', such as was done by Pablo Casals. Mendelssohn and Schubert solved the balance problem admirably in their piano trios (two from each) and Schubert's 'Trout' quintet is indeed a model of what to do with the piano when playing in ensemble with string instruments.

The timbre of the pianoforte is capable of a great variety of shades and mixes well with strings, provided the player is not too egotistical. Obviously the greater the number of string instruments playing in a compact body, the smaller will be the balance problem. In Beethoven's Op. 1, No. 3 there is a passage in which a series of $\frac{6}{4}$ chords is scored for three instruments, the piano playing the middle part.

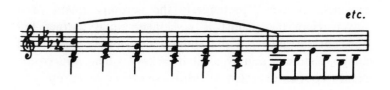

Skilfully handled by the pianist, this can sound deceptively like three string instruments.

There are good, even great, musicians who regard chamber music as an opportunity to practise sight-reading, with the inexperienced pianist stumbling through his part, hopefully reducing it to essentials and ignoring the correct and accurate pronunciation of the notes. What matter so long as one enjoys it? There may be some merit in this; there certainly was at the time of our forefathers, who made what they considered music, in their homes and for their own consumption, enthusiastically albeit rather badly. But today, the changed world being what it is, a different standard prevails in chamber music. Painstaking rehearsal, sometimes even bitter argument before unanimity on questions of tempo and balance is reached, have become recognized necessary prerequisites of presentable chamber music performance – just as much as the practising of a soloist or the rehearsals of a great orchestra under a great conductor. Sight-reading is good (when it is good) but thorough rehearsal is better. Pianists should practise their 'tricky' passages at home before questions of ensemble technique come up for discussion at rehearsal.

I am sure that the standard of performance of some of our great string quartets, piano trios and the like – not improvised *ad hoc* ensembles but permanent units of like-minded musicians performing great music – would convince even Franz Liszt that '*Kammermusik*' is not always '*Jammermusik*'.

Piano and voice

The essential difference between chamber music and accompaniment is clear, particularly the accompaniment of a singer. Here the pianist is no longer equal partner but obedient servant, and the singer's decision in matters of tempo, character and even pitch (=key) is final. Indeed the pianist is often expected to transpose a song or an operatic excerpt at sight into remote keys, so as to accommodate the singer's vocal chords. This anomaly has persisted for centuries, and apparently nothing can be done about it. The pianist who wants to accompany singers will have to undergo training in skills like the one just mentioned, and will get very little thanks for his effort. But the pleasure of hearing the sound of a beautiful voice, and of complementing that sound with his own handling of the piano part (for voice and pianoforte mix well, perhaps better than other instruments and pianoforte), in the music of great masters like Schubert, Schumann, Wolf, Liszt and Debussy, should compensate the pianist-musician for the slight personality sacrifice involved.

Nor is this sacrifice an irrevocable rule. Many of the German composers of *lieder* have given the piano long evocative solo passages when it communicates many things the voice remains silent about; here the accompanist carries the drama forward all by himself, and for this he needs to be a real artist. And it goes without saying that in certain songs by Schubert, Schumann, Wolf and others he also needs to be a first-class virtuoso.

The concerto

Let us pass on to the concerto, perhaps the most perfect combination of pianoforte and other instruments. Mozart is rightly regarded as the model in this art form. The pianoforte – very much *primus inter pares* – shows off its paces, it sparkles like precious stone, it sings, dances and all but flies away if handled by skilful fingers, never drowning the orchestra, nor being drowned by it.

Perhaps it sounds odd that drowning a whole orchestra by a single pianoforte should be possible at all. But let us not forget the difference in volume of the modern concert grand from the instrument Mozart composed for – a difference not entirely offset by the greater number of string players in the modern orchestra. It is obviously the woodwind, not the strings, that could be threatened by the powerful concert grand – a fleeting solo of the oboe or the bassoon should be treated with tenderness and care by the pianist, chamber music fashion.

Part Two: Playing the Piano

In recent years it has become customary to talk glibly about 'ornamenting' or 'decorating' Mozart's piano parts, particularly the slow movements where Mozart seems to have put only the barest minimum of notes into the score, tacitly inviting the player to exercise his imagination in inventing embellishment.

There is no doubt that Mozart (who composed piano concerti mostly for his own use) did decorate, sometimes quite lavishly, what appear in the score as just a few sketched-in notes, lacking density and even coherence, more of an *aide memoire* than the organized plan of action that a musical score should be. In such a case it is most certainly justified for a player endowed with sense of style and musicianship to accept Mozart's challenge, and not limit himself rigidly to the text.

This latter procedure was, incidentally, the strict rule up to the time when some German professor made the epoch-making discovery that Mozart played his text with improvised variations (i.e. embellishments) and it is not without amusement to ponder that before the above-mentioned discovery the scores were in fact followed rigidly and any kind of deviation from the text was castigated as a crime against the Holy Classics.

An example of the probable way such embellishments went can be found in an early edition of the Piano Sonata in F (K. 332), which is believed to contain Mozart's own variations for the slow movement, and gives instructive insight into the way similar slow movements of the concerti can and should be treated. Caution, however! It is easy to lapse from good taste; easy, too, to lose sight of the fact that the sustaining power of the twentieth-century concert grand needs much less decoration in order to fill in time between the notes of a slowly unfolding melodic line than Mozart's instrument with its short-lived sound.

Beethoven's five concerti are perhaps less perfectly balanced than Mozart's – in accordance with the different human characters of the two masters. And since, as a result, there are frequently to be found problems for the player, great maturity of judgement is required, unerring taste and instinct tempered by knowledge. There are some impossible dynamic markings, as when the bassoon is given the tune marked piano, while the pianoforte is asked to pound out an accompaniment fortissimo. The Concerto in G Major and the 'Emperor' Concerto, great and majestic works of art, abound in such absurdities. A deeper study of the period might reveal that Beethoven's bassoon was a powerful big-toned instrument, while the pianoforte, still in its infancy, had to be marked forte to be heard at all. But even without knowledge of this kind, our modern pianist has only to use his ear to know how and where Beethoven's markings must be adapted to benefit these wonderful scores. And a sympathetic conductor is, of course, essential.

The advent of the romantic age changed the character of the piano concerto. The solo instrument became absolute ruler. The 'concerto' ceased to be a piece of 'concerted' music, a musical democracy. Instead it became a dictatorship of the piano, with the pianist making all the decisions about tempo, character and balance of sound, and all too often showing a disregard of musical sense in the egotistical use of this power to display his skill. Such are the concerti of Chopin, Weber, Mendelssohn, Tschaikovsky and Rachmaninov (*inter alia*) while Brahms and Liszt tried, in their different ways, to restore to the concerto its symphonic dignity.

Schumann was a piano composer *par excellence*, even in his songs. Yet he has created a perfectly balanced concerto where, perhaps inspired by his love of the piano, he has made the orchestra also sound beautiful, though in his symphonies and overtures it tends to be a bit stiff and unnatural.

The style of the post-Lisztian concerto is still open to debate, and it is early days to take sides. The artist whose sympathies lie with the percussive type of piano writing will be at home in Bartok's first and second piano concerti while the third, more conciliatory than its aggressive predecessors, will appeal to those still longing for the beauties of a bygone age. And the concerti of Prokofiev and Stravinsky, along with the rest of their work, are too controversial to be included in the limited scope of this study.

Music for two pianos and duets

One combination of the piano with other instruments still to be mentioned is that of a piano with another piano. Not such a rarity after all, since Bach, Mozart, Schumann, Brahms and Liszt all contributed to this art form. The challenge has been taken up by excellent teams of pianists, soloists in their own right, who seem to prefer to fight the battle of wits (and against heavy odds) which is the musical life of two-piano teams. The sound can be very thick and heavy, particularly bottom-heavy and the balance must be carefully worked out and endlessly rehearsed by the two players who will be both conductors and orchestra at the same time. Mozart's Sonata in D is the perfect solution to the sound problem posed by two pianos playing simultaneously: the melodic and accompanying elements are impartially distributed, first and second pianos being first and second only in name.

If two-piano music is typically 'concert' music, at its best in the concert hall, the 'duet for four hands', played on one instrument by two players, is essentially 'house' music, originally devised for music lovers of long ago. For, before the days of gramophone and radio, those who were unable to hear symphony or chamber music concerts used these four-hand arrangements to make the acquaintance of, let us say, Beethoven's symphonies, or Haydn's string quartets.

Let us not despise these sight-reading amateurs. Stumbling through such make-shift arrangements, even if it is a poorish effort and not much of a performance, has yet given many of us a more intimate and lasting knowledge of the works in question than the easy way, now in sole use, of listening to perfect renderings on fine gramophone records. And it must be emphasized in defence of this type of musical entertainment that such masters as Mozart and Schubert have composed some of their greatest music 'for pianoforte, four hands'.

Twelve
A Note On Mechanical Reproduction

A famous pianist once came to the recording studio for the purpose of recording Chopin's octave study in B minor (Op. 25 No. 10). The maestro, with plenty of time at his disposal, decided to devote as much time as necessary to this arduous piece, and proceeded as follows: he recorded the first six octaves (very fast, of course), then paused, rested himself, recorded the next six notes, paused and rested again, and so on – repeating each six-note fragment as many times as was necessary to ensure there was not a single fault, wrong note or unwanted noise. About halfway through he went home to have a good night's sleep, and came back next day, bathed, shaved and breakfasted, to finish his performance, never once changing his method. When the tape was finished the 'editing' took even longer than the recording, because not only did choices have to be made from amongst the hundreds of dud shots, but also the pauses had to be cut out. When this *chef d'oeuvre* of editing was done, the result was stunning: the press unanimously acclaimed the maestro and his torrent of fantastic octave playing, the like of which had never been heard before.

This little story shows the good and the bad of mechanical reproduction in a distorting mirror. On the one hand we can get mechanical perfection; on the other much of the human element (of which imperfection must be an integral part) is lost in the process. Broadcasting, which is almost never 'live' today, television, gramophone – they can and do make us seem faultless, if somewhat clinical in our snow-white perfection; but does the artist really want to be remembered as an inhuman machine who never played a wrong note, or would he, on the whole, prefer the portrait to be more like himself, warts and all? After all, future generations, on receiving these dry and clean products, are hardly likely to be impressed by their artistic merits. And certainly more scope should be given to individuality, and less to an almost neurotic obsession, seemingly driving artists, mechanics, and all concerned in this machine-mad trade, into a maniacal and hopeless competition with the machine.

I have said elsewhere in this book that there may be a time coming when very good records will be made without anyone playing. Already the time has come when generations of young pianists grow up who rarely go to hear a concert. Nurtured on gramophone records, tape recordings and other mechanical surrogates, many of them have forgotten (if they ever knew it) the sound of good piano playing. Instead they imitate, in their own playing, the sound of a gramophone!

But mechanical reproduction, provided it remains faithful to Art, could be a blessing and a source of infinite delight. If recording had been invented a hundred years or so earlier we might today know exactly how Beethoven interpreted his own sonatas – and what a mass of tedious discussion about the 'classical style' would we be spared!

Recording should not be regarded as an occasion to make drastic changes in either style or technique. In the early days of recording pedalling was rather discouraged. Of this restriction there remains to this day a very slight trace, only as much as a 'be cautious' warning, for bad pedalling becomes more noticeable on a recording than in a drawing room, but not more noticeable than in a resonant concert hall. The fact is that bad pedalling is intolerable in all manner of conditions, and recording is no exception. The difference in nuisance value lies in the fact that this type of crime, committed in a public concert, is forgotten when the concert is over, whereas a recording is heard again and again by the enthusiast who discovers more and more faults in it.

However, clean phrasing is recommended and too slow or too fast tempi are to be avoided. Excesses in this field, sometimes tolerable on the concert platform, tend to become blatant on a record. It is also wise to avoid harsh percussive playing, as this can wreck a recording mechanically. In these respects, then, concessions do have to be made to the medium.

As for the instrument itself, ideally the recording artist should choose one with easy action, otherwise the job may prove too strenuous physically. It is not necessary to treat the piano in any special way mechanically, but care should be taken about faultless tuning, for every buzz and waver tells painfully on a record. If possible a good tuner should be in permanent attendance during a session, and frequent re-tuning is advisable.

A once popular scientific joke, transferred to the field of piano recording – namely, that a hundred monkeys strumming on a hundred pianos for a sufficient number of years (one million if necessary) will have strummed out in the end all the works of Beethoven – has a nasty smell of truth about it when one thinks about the conditions in which recordings are made.

If we want to save mechanical reproduction for the purpose of disseminating art, we need real artists, with artistic purpose – not strumming monkeys proving, or disproving, the Law of Averages. My appeal to artists is: make as many fine records as possible, and beat the monkeys!

Part Three:

The Great
Pianoforte Composers

Thirteen
Beethoven: the thirty-two piano sonatas

Let us imagine that a man from Mars is wafted on to our planet, and let us further imagine that he has the curiosity to explore our civilization in depth. Having examined what we consider the most valuable of our achievements, our visitor may wish to find the one single jewel, if possible the crowning glory of this civilization, the one sample typical of man's endeavour which he could put into his luggage and take back to his planet. Should he wish to do so, I would undoubtedly recommend Beethoven's thirty-two piano sonatas for that purpose.

No doubt many people will disagree and possibly maintain that the Bible or the works of Shakespeare (or Dante, or Goethe) or some great painting have a greater claim to represent European civilization at its finest and most typical. My advocacy of the Beethoven piano sonatas rests not merely on the fact that I happen to be a musician and that the present book is about the pianoforte, but also that musical – unlike literary masterpieces, which are surrounded by linguistic barriers – present a language accessible to all. Moreover music deals more readily than its sister arts with emotion, which it at once expresses and conceals. Thus, music can be said to be a revelation and also a mystery.

Art cannot exist without form. This means, not that what the artist has to say must be said in the way some other artist has said something else in a previous age – this is the traditional, academic view of form – but rather that the will to express creates its own form, intrinsic to what is to be expressed. The artist's stature is measured not so much by the 'what' as by the 'how'. Thus form becomes creation, and creation becomes form. The mere facile inventor of tunes cannot claim to be a composer.

The essence of Beethoven – perhaps the greatest artist ever produced by human civilization – lies distilled in the piano sonatas. Here form and content are unfailingly in harmony – the hallmark of great art. Mozart's different, and possibly even more flawless, perfection is a little less human and a little more rooted in one particular age, while Beethoven's humanity is ageless.

The sonatas in general

Let us now look at these works, not indeed in great detail but rather in the way one walks through an old and marvellous garden, admiring a proliferation of unprecedented richness.

The gardener who created it was in no way a specialist. The student who wishes to come to a *full* understanding of Beethoven's piano sonatas must also make himself familiar with the symphonies, the string quartets and other chamber music, the great works in concerto form, and the rest of the piano music. Nevertheless Beethoven, who, like Mozart, was able to compose several different works simultaneously, seems to have been at work on a piano sonata at any given moment of his creative life. In other words, whatever else occupied his mind – opera, symphony or cantata – there were always sketches for yet another piano sonata lurking somewhere on his writing desk; and Beethoven's plans were nearly always carried out, no matter how slow and laborious the way from sketch to finished product. For Beethoven was not a fast worker; unlike Mozart he did not work out a whole sonata or symphony, down to the very last detail, in his head before he put pen to paper, making the final writing-down a mere process of copying out (Mozart could do this while listening to conversation going on around him); on the contrary, Beethoven fought all his battles with God's Angel on paper, so to speak, leaving his sketches behind after his death, for all the world to see. Innumerable erasures, improvements, new beginnings, the whole difficult process of gestation and birth, can be followed from these sketch books – to the student of Beethoven, even though he may not know the ultimate products, they are human documents of shattering impact.

But it is not right to speak of Beethoven as a 'constipated' composer lacking the spontaneous melody of a Mozart or a Schubert. It is true that, when he was visited by an inspiration, his perfectionism made him try many different ways of developing the germ idea, until his method of polishing, pruning, condensing and deepening led him by stages to the final form of the idea, the form that seemed to his severely critical mind at last suitable to constitute the thematic material of a great musical creation. But – and this must be emphasized – the original germ idea was every bit as spontaneous as those of the greatest melodists. The labours of Hercules (of which the sketch books tell, and of which traces can be found even in the works themselves) bear witness, not to any lack of inspiration, but to a stubborn artistic integrity, bordering on obsession, and a ruthless self-criticism that had to be satisfied first and foremost. We know nothing of Mozart's creative processes because it was his method to hide them, giving the world only the finished (and perfect) product.

Thus the main difference between the two great masters seems to be this: Beethoven lets us into all his secrets. The drama of creation is enacted under our eyes. Mozart's curtain rises when that drama is over. How much bitter stress and agony went into the composition of Mozart's Piano Concerto in C Minor or of his Symphony in G Minor we shall probably never know.

It must be obvious by now that, when I speak of the agony of creation in Beethoven, I do not mean the sketch books only. The agony is there, in the very music, regardless of what we may call the 'character' of that music. Beethoven at his gayest, most optimistic, shows his battle scars: his touch is heavier, his gait more ponderous than Mozart's who, even in his most tragic moments, remains light and gracious. This is perhaps the price that Beethoven the artist paid for extracting his precious ore from soil made fertile by the sufferings of Beethoven the man. Would we have had as great music from Beethoven had he been a happy human being?

The biographical significance of the sonatas

Beethoven composed his thirty-two piano sonatas during a creative life that was, by present-day standards, a short one: he was twenty-six years old when the first three sonatas were published and survived the publication of the last piano sonata, Op. 111, by only five years – a span of about thirty-one years. Because this works out as an average of one sonata each year or thereabouts, it is not perhaps too far-fetched to assign some sort of autobiographical meaning to the sonatas – indeed it is quite tempting to do so. Not, of course, in the sense of expecting the music to be descriptive of actual events in Beethoven's life, though there is one example of this: the sonata entitled 'Les Adieux' (Op. 81a), but in the deeper sense, that of recognizing how the sonatas represent distinctive stages of the artist's inner life – in this sense I think we are entitled to an interpretation of the whole vast complex as an autobiography in music.

Liszt, in the B minor Sonata and other major works, gave us self-portraits of astonishing verisimilitude, albeit the face we look at is always the same. Beethoven recorded all the phases of his human and artistic evolution in works of compelling strength and diversity – in fact he gave us the story of his life. In this, as in many other things, he stands alone among composers. Not unconnected with this is the fact that all his piano sonatas are so different one from another.

It is necessary at this point to glance for a moment at another great composer of piano sonatas – Beethoven's forerunner and erstwhile teacher, Haydn. The sonatas of this master, some of which are full of wit, originality and charm as well as technical perfection in the handling of the sonata form, have yet the undeniable fault of 'sameness', of being cut to the same measurements. No doubt these measurements are very elegant indeed (even if the harpsichord style of Scarlatti and the Mannheim composers may obtrude a little), but perhaps this similarity of mould and the consequent slight aura of dullness surrounding these sonatas explain why only a few out of the many have survived the revolutionary change-over from harpsichord to pianoforte. Haydn was not whole-hearted in welcoming this change, unlike Mozart, whose use of the harpsichord was virtually limited to the *secco recitative* of his operas. Mozart's piano sonatas, more than Haydn's, were piano music *pure sang* but not perhaps Mozart at his greatest – this was reserved for the concerti. It was left to Beethoven to break away radically from the harpsichord – not without paying lip-service to it by labelling early sonatas 'For harpsichord or pianoforte' – and finally to compose sonatas for the '*Hammerclavier*'.

The astonishing change from Haydn and Mozart to Beethoven, in the way of using the piano not as a substitute for the harpsichord but as a new instrument with new possibilities, a change that is clearly noticeable in the first three sonatas (Op. 2, dedicated to Haydn), could be partly ascribed to the influence of another hitherto neglected master: Muzio Clementi. Clementi was a brilliant pianist, like Mozart and Beethoven, and like almost every pianist-composer since time immemorial he fashioned his piano style to suit his technique. The brilliance of Beethoven's early keyboard music undoubtedly owes something to this great musician, whom Mozart mistakenly dismissed as a heartless technician (though he did not disdain to use the theme of one of Clementi's sonatas in his own 'Magic Flute' overture). Clementi's piano sonatas are unjustly neglected; valuable in themselves, they are more valuable still by the influence they had on such widely separated composers as Beethoven and Chopin. (More about Clementi in Chapter 14.)

But to discern the influence of earlier composers on one so much greater than they is not to explain his greatness (which cannot be so explained) but, rather, to bring it down to a lower level – nearer to our own understanding perhaps. Indeed it is only through laying bare the roots that one can hope to begin to comprehend the process whereby the mighty tree came to grow so tall. All history, and most of the history of music, seems to consist of conclusions arrived at by this sort of method. But let no one be in doubt: beauty and genius cannot be genealogically analysed; only their surfaces yield something to the searching intellect. Genius absorbs all outside influences but converts them into a beauty all its own.

Sonata form

Having established that these thirty-two sonatas, representing phases of Beethoven's inner evolution, are as different from one another as is consistent with their coming from the same source, we are now about to discover that even the movements of the sonatas differ from each other. It would seem as if Beethoven had deliberately set himself the task of never repeating anything – no two slow movements, no two minuets or scherzi, are alike. Presently we must look at some of the sonatas from the instrumentalist's point of view, but without excluding the musician from the operation. The musician is aware, of course, of the meaning of the term 'sonata form' so a short outline will be sufficient.

Sonata form is simply an extended version of the so-called ternary song form (ABA) the essentials of which – a first theme (A) followed by a second idea (B) followed by a return or recapitulation of (A) – are maintained but broadened in the following way. Instead of a simple melodic idea of, say, eight or sixteen bars, we have a whole group of themes (at least two contrasting in character and tonality), this group of themes being called the 'exposition'. This is followed by a 'development' section (the B of the ternary form), then the A (exposition) section returns, both first and second themes, but with the key relations changed in favour of the tonic key which now preponderates, this section being called 'recapitulation'. First and second themes (= subjects) are recognizable in the exposition by their tonic-dominant (or in minor keys, tonic-relative major) relationships which, as I have said above, are cancelled in the recapitulation where everything appears in the tonic. The development is a freely modulating fantasy, based on thematic material heard in the exposition.

Perhaps it is not superfluous to remind the young pianist trying to interpret a Beethoven sonata of this 'dry and uninspiring' thing, the sonata form, or to insist that the knowledge of keyboard harmony, or just simply harmony, is essential to his understanding of music. Dry and uninspiring? But if we consider the vast catalogue of works in which the great classical masters expressed themselves in this, their most natural way (and Beethoven, for all his innovations, was no exception), we realize how much more important it is to know not only the rules but also the thousand subtle ways in which Beethoven used the rules – and broke them to be sure – than all the daily finger exercises at the keyboard.

The discipline of sonata form lent frame to some of the most sublime music in the world – how could it possibly be dismissed as dry and uninspiring? It goes without saying that in a cyclical work like a sonata the term 'sonata form' usually refers to the form of the first movement. The middle movements, more often than not, show the features of the ABA song form (binary or ternary) and very often a combination of two such forms, the second one being called 'Trio' for reasons not necessary to go into; after the trio the complete first ABA is brought back unchanged, the composer's request to this effect being the marking 'Da Capo' or D.C. During the 'Da Capo' any repeat signs are cancelled (should there have been any) unless otherwise indicated. The last movements of sonatas are frequently written in rondo form and are often called by the name 'rondo'. The more primitive kind of rondo consists of a theme alternating with episodes ABACAD etc. The more sophisticated rondo – frequent in Beethoven – is a combination of sonata and rondo form. A short analytical scrutiny of some of these rondos will show the student for himself how this fusion is effected.

111

The early period

The first three of the thirty-two piano sonatas show the young Beethoven: strong, bold, confident and sure of his powers, not least of his powers as a brilliant pianist. If he composed these Op. 2 sonatas as a vehicle to display his own skill to the elegant Viennese nobility, in whose circles the young man, newly arrived from Bonn, was soon to gain a foothold, he could not have made a better choice. The third one, in C major, especially shows the young virtuoso at his most flamboyant. No. 2 in A major seems more profound without being less pianistic. This is a far cry from Haydn or Mozart but not so far from Clementi. Only No. 1 in F minor has a few Haydnesque features. The piano writing is leaner than that of the other two sonatas but by no means easy. It is an interesting fact that, when Beethoven issued a whole set of sonatas (usually three, sometimes two, together), they lent themselves, by the disposition of their tonalities and characters, to being performed together. And a further interesting fact is that they are practically never so performed.

The next sonata, Op. 7 in E flat, is known as the 'amorous' sonata, perhaps because the last two movements really have something of the young man in love. But the greatest movement of this sonata is undoubtedly the 'Largo con gran' espressione' – so eloquent and appealing that it belies its C major tonality (a key that can sometimes sound hard and dry).

Op. 10 is another set of three sonatas, in C minor, F major and D major respectively. Beethoven's individuality shines through the somewhat Haydnesque exterior, shown particularly in the last movement of the Sonata in F major. The Sonata in D major has another of those great slow movements which belong by no means exclusively to the 'late' period: this D minor Largo has a unique intensity and is one of the high points of Beethoven's early period. The C minor Sonata of this group, sometimes called the 'little Pathétique' (perhaps because of the key), makes no revolutionary break-away from convention, perhaps less than

Mozart's sonata in the same key, but is a remarkably good 'key' to Beethoven's style, a gate through which the student may enter this world better than through any other.

As far as the general disposition of the early sonatas is concerned, we have already seen several sonatas with four movements, an innovation of Beethoven's. Of course four-movement works abound among the string quartets, symphonies and other works of Mozart, and Haydn also, but not, oddly enough, among the piano sonatas; in this field Beethoven seems to have been the first to add a minuet or scherzo to the three-movement scheme. Another innovation is the allegro or allegretto – as Op. 7 or Op. 10 No. 2 – which is neither minuet nor scherzo, nor indeed slow movement, but which partakes of some of the characteristics of all three. There are many examples of this in the sonatas – a Beethoven hallmark *par excellence*. The scherzi are mostly in $\frac{3}{4}$ time, and clearly reveal their derivation from the minuet. The dividing line is not very marked, neither is the evolution from the one to the other uninterrupted. The Sonata in F Minor, Op. 2, has a minuet which is to all intents and purposes a scherzo (it has, accordingly, to be taken at a fairly quick tempo), but in the next sonata there is a scherzo which is more like a minuet both in speed and character. Beethoven's scherzi, on the whole, do not amount to a final discarding of the old minuet, which reappears from time to time in later works. Anyone with ears to hear will notice that many of Beethoven's scherzi are by no means jocular or else the humour is of a rather grim and caustic kind, but this feature is less noticeable in the early sonatas. The reader will see that in this one respect at least (in omitting from the scherzo the very thing that gave it it's name: the joke), Beethoven was forerunner to a composer who admired him only with reservations: Chopin.

The popular 'Pathétique', Op. 13, marks yet another important step in Beethoven's evolution: there is no longer any trace of influence from Haydn or Mozart. It is as if this wonderful youth, bursting with strength and optimism, had become the fully-grown Beethoven, marked already by the darker aspects of life. Tragic undertones are beginning to creep in: a melancholy or nostalgia in the Rondo movement (which was originally conceived for a violin sonata) persists to the end, and cheerfulness does not succeed in breaking in. The slow introduction to the first movement is thematically closely connected with the movement itself, not a detachable adjunct to it; and the heavenly Adagio, perhaps not as profound as other slow movements in other sonatas, is yet proof of Beethoven's gift of spontaneous melody, disputed by some critics.

Op. 14 consists of two short sonatas in E and G respectively, remarkable in that No. 1 has one of the above mentioned allegretto movements so typical of Beethoven (and which, according to his pupils, he used to play at a 'furious speed'), and that No. 2 in G was the subject of one of Beethoven's rare comments on his own music – a comment to the effect that the opening movement was a dialogue between a man and a woman. Allusions to a 'masculine' and a 'feminine' principle crop up frequently in commentaries on Beethoven's works – and not only in dealing with this particular sonata – and there is no doubt that this line of analysis originated from Beethoven himself. For the rest, the charm and contentment evoked by these two short works require no further comment from me, except perhaps the expression of a slight doubt in the matter of chronology – could these sonatas have been composed before and not after the tragic 'Pathetique'? His pupil Schindler, a diligent scholar, has left a most interesting bar-by-bar description of how Beethoven played the Op. 14 sonatas which Thayer quotes in his Beethoven book and which I recommend students to read carefully, not indeed with a view to imitating every detail slavishly ('here Beethoven accelerated the tempo a good deal . . . here he held a note extremely long . . .') but to absorb the spirit of fanatical insistence on expression and freedom that must have imbued Beethoven's style of interpretation: he put expression far above accuracy and formalistic perfection.

A slight digression here on the much discussed subject of the 'classical' style of interpretation seems not out of place. What platform artist, exposed to attacks by well-meaning but misguided critical indignation, has not experienced the onslaught of self-appointed guardians of the so-called classical style? What student has not suffered similar injuries from teachers who ought to know better? The basis of this philosophy is a pedantic and ludicrous exclusion of any originality or spontaneity in the matter of deviation from metronomic time-keeping, that flexibility mis-named 'rubato' and held in horror by these modern Beckmessers which was an integral part of the great nineteenth-century pianists' interpretation. The results of this deplorable kind of indoctrination are heard only too frequently in our concert halls, and are approved by some of our critics. They are extremely dull and out of touch with living music, which they reduce to some sort of intellectual paper game.

I myself heard Pablo Casals – one of the greatest interpreters of the classics – say that the greatest crimes against the spirit of music were committed in the name of the classical style.

But let us return to our sonatas. The next two in chronological order (Op. 22 in B flat and Op. 26 in A flat) share the privilege of being out of popular favour – the earlier one was never a popular favourite, the later one had this distinction for a while then lost it – but any unbiased judge will admit their solid worth for all that. The Op. 22 sonata especially, fashioned in a masterly way – all substance, no padding, not an ounce of superfluous flesh – should be performed more often. It is hard to guess why it is not: perhaps because its mood is one of untroubled optimism, and we are conditioned to think of Beethoven as a 'tragic' composer? It is perhaps for this reason also that the Op. 26, which includes the once famous Funeral March 'Sulla Morte d'un Eroe' ('On the Death of a Hero'), enjoyed quite a long run in the early 1900s. Besides the Funeral March (an unconventional feature in a sonata) there is also an unusual first movement, a set of beautiful variations on an andante theme, thus making two 'slow movements' in all – but in this Beethoven had a forerunner in Mozart's Sonata in A Major. The Finale, coming immediately after the Funeral March, is something of an oddity, and has puzzled the seekers of psychological clues: here Beethoven has composed a totally objective piece of perpetual motion, leaving all sentiment on one side. It is almost like a study by J. B. Cramer. It is as if Beethoven were making a mocking gesture towards commentators who expect further tragic profundities after the Funeral March. We shall see that Chopin, faced with a similar problem in his Sonata in B Flat Minor, also chose to follow up the Funeral March with a movement of motoric character – but one that has a ghostly and terrifying graveyard atmosphere. If Beethoven were thinking of ghosts they were certainly very friendly ones – more like neighbours gossiping after the funeral.

Next on our list are two works sub-titled 'Quasi una Fantasia', Op. 27. Beethoven indicates by this sub-title that liberties will be taken with the conventional structure of the sonata. The unusual thing about the Sonata in E Flat Major – the first of the two – is that it must be played without interruption, although it is not a one-movement work but clearly articulated into four distinct movements. Perhaps it is far-fetched to see in this work a forerunner of Schubert's 'Wanderer' Fantasy (which, however, it might conceivably have inspired to some extent) because the thematic unity of the Schubert work is not attempted. There is, at all events, a very successfully accomplished 'unity in diversity' in this lovely sonata – further accentuated by a most apposite quote from the slow movement just before the end. In the first movement I see Beethoven's incredible power to fashion a coherent whole from a series of seemingly self-contained sections of eight or sixteen bars – a task no other composer could have accomplished. Only the Finale of this sonata is in sonata form.

If this sonata is perhaps more objective in utterance and also more contrapuntal in texture than some of its predecessors, in the second sonata of this Op. 27, nicknamed the 'Moonlight' Sonata (but let us not go into the area of sentimental slush where this nickname originated), we have a work both totally subjective and totally homophonous. It starts with an 'Adagio sostenuto' of heart-rending plaintiveness, and let us not deceive ourselves into thinking its performance easy. A consolatory Allegretto follows (not a scherzo nor a minuet, but the mixture of Beethoven's own brand already mentioned) and is quickly obliterated by a dark, stormy Finale, with surging arpeggios culminating in a couple of crashing chords, all this adding up to a very novel kind of theme and a very novel kind of Finale. If the word 'romantic' has any meaning at all, then surely this is a romantic work: it proves that Beethoven was, *inter alia*, a romantic composer.

That he was other things as well is proved by the sonata immediately following, Op. 28 in D Major, sometimes called (but not by the composer) the 'Pastoral'. The name is not altogether ill-chosen; the last movement especially, with its rocking ⁶⁄₈ rhythm, makes the kind of 'nature sounds' with which lovers of the Pastoral Symphony are familiar. An interesting feature of this work is the copious use of the Pedal Point – and another, probably arrived at involuntarily but which is nevertheless a witness to Beethoven's instinct for unity, is a certain similarity in the interval sequences in which all the main themes are built. The sequence 1-5-4-3-2-1 is repeated over and over again, but creates melodic shapes of great diversity. I will quote passages from all four movements to illustrate my point. These quotes are not

117

Scherzo (Trio)

Finale

etc.

just passing episodes, but actually the main thematic material on which each of the movements (except the Scherzo) is built. Accident? Possibly, but the kind of accident that only happens to a Beethoven.

The middle period

It has become too easily accepted as axiomatic in the recent research into Beethoven to divide the Master's creative life into three periods: early, middle and late. This simplification does not fit the facts if we examine them closely. Beethoven's dictum, 'I am dissatisfied with my work: I will seek new paths', does not necessarily signify a sudden decision taken just before he composed his Op. 31 sonatas, or other works of that moment in time. Nor does it signify a wholesale repudiation of all that had gone before. The 'new paths' were found little by little, and the more Beethovenish Beethoven who finally emerged (at least, according to the simplifiers) is already foreshadowed in some of the 'early' sonatas. Nor is the line of evolution straight and unequivocal: relapses occur – if we wish to call them so – or else one suspects that the scene is principally laid in other fields at the moment in question (string quartet, symphony, concerto), the piano sonata as such receiving only faint echoes of a battle raging elsewhere. Indeed there is, I believe, no fundamental difference in outlook between the 'early' Pastoral sonata and the allegedly middle period sonata in G, Op. 31, No. 1.

True, the last page of this delightful work suddenly blossoms out in a coda section full of surprises, where Beethoven seems to improvise a cadenza, beginning, in true concerto tradition, on the $\substack{6 \\ 4}$ chord which always heralds that kind of enterprise; but such surprises were not unknown to those who heard the young Beethoven improvise in the drawing rooms of the Viennese nobility. As for the other movements, in the highly ornamented Adagio Beethoven seems to make a polite bow towards the already fashionable Rossini, and there is not much in the otherwise delicious first movement to justify talk of 'new paths'.

There is plenty in the Sonata in D Minor, the next of the set, where the romantic Beethoven of the 'Moonlight' and the 'Pathétique' reappears but somehow more agitated and anguished, with a far freer range of modulation; in the first movement the dramatic device of the recitative is invoked – a stunning moment undoubtedly, but one remembers that the instrumental recitative is not rare in Bach's keyboard music nor in Mozart's – and the pedal is given an important part in the evocation of a ghostly kind of sound effect ('as if spoken in an empty vault' was Beethoven's instruction, so often disregarded by pianists who know better and tend to ascribe such oddities to Beethoven's incipient deafness). After the sombre first movement, the Adagio with its remarkably far-flung melodic line – these are new paths indeed – seems to breathe peace and contentment, while the Finale, sweetly rocking and belligerently storming by turns, exploits the dolcissimo shades of the pianoforte most beautifully. This movement is by far the most original of the three. Far from the conventional rondo of the age (it is written in sonata form) it is a close relation, or forerunner, of that greater finale, the last movement of the great A minor string quartet. It should not be played too fast or too 'brilliantly' but more like a wistful farewell to Youth.

The last sonata of this set of three, in E flat, is by contrast full of sunshine and strength. Beethoven wrote brilliantly for the piano (one is almost tempted to say 'for the pianist') from the beginning, but by this time the growth of the instrument (both in volume and compass) gave him more scope than ever before. In this sonata he is really seen flexing his muscles, especially in that fiery tarantella, the Finale. The disposition of the movements is unusual. There is a great Scherzo, in $\frac{2}{4}$ time and sonata form, but no real slow movement, its place being taken by a Minuet of touching simplicity which, like the Adagio of the 'Pathétique', gives the lie to those who deny Beethoven the gift of spontaneous, heartfelt melody. Both these middle movements are perfect gems of inspired craftsmanship. The opening movement, a fine example of what Wagner called the 'singing Allegro', makes high demands on the digital skill of the performer, as does the rest of the sonata – and almost all sonatas from now on.

For we have come, almost without noticing it, to Beethoven's period of 'sheer virtuosity'. A giant strength, happily conscious of itself and of what it can do, is giving itself full rein during this period: the instrument must yield its utmost. New pianistic devices abound: glissandi in octaves, wide leaps, double thirds and sixths, full chords in succession. If Beethoven did later make the contemptuous remark, so often quoted, about the 'miserable instrument' being far from his thoughts when he composed – the time for such contempt was yet to come. Three sonatas of this period (Op. 53, 54, 57) bear witness to Beethoven's preoccupation with pianistic bravura – yes and display. From here to Liszt is not such a very long way, and only a matter of a few more years. But first we must pass, on our way, the two charming 'Sonatinas', both in G, Op. 49. They are early works, possibly composed even before the Op. 2 sonatas – who knows what accident or publisher's waywardness brought them into their present place amongst the sonatas? – but they are by no means negligible, and should not be thrown to beginners, as they so often are. The minuet theme of the second sonatina is used – with greater effect – in the still popular Septet in E flat.

The 'Waldstein Sonata', Op. 53, is too well-known and too often performed to need any comment beyond the general one, already made, on Beethoven's display of brilliance. Of course there is a lot more in it than that. One of the conspicuous features of this period – the enormously enlarged coda section, amounting almost to a second development (which is very much an item Beethoven added to the sonata form in those wanderings on 'new paths') – is in evidence in both the first and last movements. To this should be added that there is no slow movement in this two-movement sonata: only a slow 'introduction' ('intermezzo' would be a better name for it) separates the two fast movements; and that Beethoven did originally intend an Andante in F Major, which was composed and then thrown out, probably because of the excessive length to which the sonata would have swollen by its inclusion. This Andante was later published as a separate piece entitled *Andante Favori*. The Waldstein Sonata was, if we accept Beethoven's description of the Adagio as an introduction to the Rondo, the first of the great two-movement sonatas (not counting, of course, the Op. 49 sonatinas), the last, and greatest, being Op. 111.

The 'Waldstein' is followed hard on its heels by another two-movement work, in F, Op. 54. Beethoven avoids, here as almost everywhere, the conventional, the already tried out. The result is something that could be, and has been, called 'two characteristic pieces', a Minuet and a Toccata. Only both are written in a modified sonata form and extended to sonata proportions. The Minuet movement's contrasting second subject is only symbolically present (through the key of C major) and is embedded in a long octave passage of considerable pianistic bravura – this octave passage starts off as a 'bridge', continues as a Second Subject, and after a rest for breathing constitutes also the development section of this very interesting sonata form; it then reappears very much curtailed in the recapitulation only to give way to a much needed extended coda section in which the main theme is commented upon by brilliant passages and finally rounded off in a calm and beautiful ending. The toccata-like second movement is an example of the sustained perpetual-motion type of motoric music of great brilliance; it is, like the first

121

movement of this sonata, written in sonata form, with an exposition so short as to be rudimentary, and an enormously enlarged development, mostly shimmering modulation and shimmering sound.

If the Op. 54 shows Beethoven at his least romantic or most objective, with the stress on craftsmanship rather than sentiment, in the next sonata (known as the 'Appassionata') we see him returning to the romantic fold with a vengeance. This work (in F minor, Op. 57), well-known, well-loved and very much performed, has a sustained violence of utterance so subjective and Beethovenian that the listener and the performer are left breathless at the end – breathless and unaware of the enormous craftsmanship that went into this long cry of passion. The proportions are even greater than those of the 'Waldstein', the writing as homophonous as that of the 'Moonlight', and one notices the long coda sections – the new Beethoven touch added to the old sonata form. Between the two stormy movements Beethoven places an Andante with variations, a work of great simplicity (each variation ascends by an octave on the keyboard, doubling the rhythmic values as it does so) representing perhaps a moment of happiness and repose. No doubt this sonata is the most characteristic of the so-called middle period, and has so caught the imagination of Beethoven commentators that the Beethoven image – because other facets of it were disregarded – suffered some considerable distortion. It must be said that romantic Beethovenites like Romain Rolland, lavish with epithets like 'gigantic', 'titanic', 'heroic' and the like, tend to neglect the fact that in the great forest that was Beethoven (have we not compared him with a garden?) there are other trees, just as tall, but different.

The transition period

As if to prove this, Beethoven followed up the 'Appassionata' with a short, two-movement sonata in F sharp major, Op. 78. A bigger contrast cannot be imagined: the *'Sturm und Drang'* is replaced by a calm, a warmth and also a great economy in the use of pianistic resources – as if Beethoven, conscious of his strength and of his victory, had settled down (temporarily) to a comfortable enjoyment of a life where passion and struggle had very little place. This sonata – one of Beethoven's own favourites (he commended it as a work superior to the over-admired 'Moonlight') – is said to be an improvisation subsequently committed to paper. If this is true, it must be said that nothing could be less like an improvisation; and that, despite its shortness, no one could call this terse but important piece a sonatina. Its importance lies in the fact that it opens the series of 'borderline' sonatas, no longer 'middle period', not yet 'late', but going towards that rarefied spiritual atmosphere we associate with the last five piano sonatas, the inward-turning Beethoven, pre-vented by growing deafness from pursuing his virtuoso career, but helped, perhaps by the same deafness, in his ascent towards transcendental beauties greater than those others were given to penetrate. It is perhaps at this precise moment that the sonatas become more biographical (that is indicative of Beethoven's inner growth) than ever before.

Again the road is not straight and diversions occur. The next sonata, in G, Op. 79 (this one is officially called 'Sona-tina' unlike the two little sonatinas, Op. 49) has been ques-tioned by no less a person than Hans von Bülow as to wheth-er it is genuine late Beethoven or an early work accidentally carrying a late opus number. I would say that, at least in the first movement 'alla Tedesca', the hallmark of the late Beet-hoven is so unmistakable that one would almost believe the Master to be imitating himself; it sounds somewhat like one of the late Bagatelles – which is not a pejorative evaluation. In the second movement the Mendelssohn of the *Veneziani-sches Gondallier* type of music seems to be prophetically invoked; the last movement is admittedly light-weight, but as befits a sonatina: a light-hearted performance is necessary to make its charm come to life.

'Les Adieux' is the title given by Beethoven to the sonata next in chronological order (Op. 81a), and its first movement is also entitled 'Les Adieux' ('Farewell'), rather as a collection of poems or short stories is sometimes called by the name of the first piece in it; the two other titles – 'L' Absence' and 'Le Retour' – are clear enough in themselves but the music is so eloquent as to make explanation supererogatory. This is in no sense 'programme music' (not even in the limited sense of the 'Pastoral' Symphony). Beethoven uses the titles to make comprehension even easier, a courtesy towards the performer rather than the listener. He goes even further than that, by putting the word '*Lebewohl*' over the motto theme with which the introduction of the first movement opens. I know of only one other example in

Beethoven of words written in the score (words that fit the melody but are not to be sung) namely in the last movement of the last string quartet – '*Muss es sein? Es muss sein!*' – where the sense of the words is humorous. For doing the same sort of thing in his Dante Symphony and elsewhere, Liszt was bitterly attacked. And yet this device – a hint to the performer as to a hidden meaning that otherwise might have eluded him – is every bit as justified as are markings like 'dolce espressivo'. A point of interest is that this 'Fare-thee-well' motif, first heard in the Introduction, dominates the whole of the first movement, even eclipsing what is, academically speaking, the main subject. Beethoven's slow introductions frequently carry thematic material significant in the subsequent course of the work. This organic nature (first observed in the 'Pathétique') of Beethoven's intro-ductions makes it necessary, in the particular case in question, that the slow and fast speeds should be coordinated. I recommend the ratio 1:4 which means that one beat ($\flat$) of the Adagio equals one 'alla-breve' beat ($\downarrow$) of the Allegro. The Andante must have puzzled many musicians at the time it was first heard as to what key it was in, because of its restless wandering through many modulations. Beethoven himself added to the confusion by his three-flats key signature; in my opinion the initial tonality is G minor and not C minor. The beautiful, wistful Andante is simplicity itself as regards form: a concise sonata exposition recapitulated without development. The reason lies almost certainly in the prolific modulations occurring at the very beginning of the movement: a further modulatory section would needlessly make obscurity more obscure. This obscurity ends suddenly when the wandering comes to a rest on a tense, hushed chord (the dominant seventh of expectation!) and the jubilant Finale explodes like a bomb. This is yet another sonata form (not a rondo) and it is all joy and happiness and bells ringing and a moment of stillness just before the end – as if such paroxysm of bliss were too much for the human heart. The work is dedicated to the Archduke Rudolph who had befriended Beethoven generously, but one wonders if all this emotion could really be caused by the triviality of the Archduke's absence from and return to Vienna.

In the Sonata in E Minor, Op. 90, Beethoven's progress towards what is called the 'late period' continues. This masterly two-movement sonata is only half in E minor – the second and longer half being in E major – but the misnomer 'E Minor Sonata' seems ineradicable from general usage. Beethoven is said to have spoken of a masculine and a feminine principle operating in the first movement, similar to what he said about the G Major Sonata (Op. 14, No. 2) of a dialogue between a man and a woman. It is not difficult to accept this interpretation, the only slight criticism of it being that such contrast can be seen in almost all polythematic music (music based on more than one theme); indeed, unless I am mistaken, Wagner, in his work on conducting, based a lot of his interpretative ideas on this notion. However, let it pass. The beautifully shaped melodic simplicity of the

Rondo is deceptive: if you look below the Schubertian or even Mendelssohnian surface you see the complexities of contrapuntal and harmonic subtleties to come.

The late sonatas

And now we are in the middle of the 'late period', and we must accordingly talk in whispers, for we have entered the Holy of Holies. In this rarefied atmosphere we shall find prophetic glimpses into the future. They will be specially noticed in the Sonata in A Major, Op. 101, where the yearning first movement is a forewarning of Wagner's Tristan music, and of which the second movement could almost be Schumann. But in the Finale, if nowhere else, Beethoven turns towards Bach – and that is not turning towards the future but towards the past. If names of other composers are mentioned here, the implication is not of course any lack of originality; indeed this could not be the case since neither Schumann nor Wagner were yet born at the time (or perhaps only just) and the influence of Bach, far from weakening Beethoven's personality, made it even stronger. Beethoven did not find writing fugues as easy and natural as Bach, or even Mozart, and academic experts on sixteenth-century counterpoint may find faults here and there. The polyphony bears the marks of struggle (as does so much else, even simple tunes, in Beethoven). But then nothing is ever done ostentatiously at this period of Beethoven's life, nothing to display easy technical mastery; rather it is to heighten psychological tension, to build up towards tremendous climaxes, that Beethoven uses the fugue and the canon. In the marvellously constructed Finale of the Op. 101 Sonata, the fugato is embedded in the centre in place of the development section, as if to demonstrate how a seemingly homophonous theme can be contrapuntally treated – 'seemingly' homophonous because the contrapuntal potentialities of the material are there, right from the beginning of the movement, for all who have ears to hear.

It is interesting to compare the diverse ways in which the

fugal element is strategically located in the late sonatas: in Op. 101 it forms part of the Finale, as we have seen; in Op. 109 it appears as one of a set of variations; again, in the last movement in Op. 110, the fugue comes not by itself but welded together with a slow movement (a few words will be said about this later); and in the 'Hammerclavier' Sonata there is the famous, or infamous, 'Fuga a tre voci', a work of immense proportions, considered by some a Chimboraso in all music, by others an un-playable, un-pianistic monstrosity. Only the last sonata, Op. 111, has no fugue or just a short and rudimentary hint of one in the first movement.

To return to Op. 101 for another moment. After the condensed, expressive, 'Wagnerian' first movement there is a march-like (but not at all scherzo-like) second movement, the Trio section of which is, if not a regular canon in the Bachian sense, yet very canonical and introspective – after which the march is played Da Capo. A wonderful yearning introduction (or intermezzo?) leads to a short cadenza, and a few forlorn fragments from the first movement remembered in anything but tranquillity; then the anguished questioning mood is suddenly dissipated by the radiant Finale.

It is difficult to retain the chronological order of dealing with the sonatas, because one has the natural wish to leave the greatest to the last; but we must continue and, in chronological order, we have next to speak about what is undoubtedly the greatest but not the last of the sonatas. It is the one in B flat, Op. 106, known as the 'Hammerclavier' Sonata.* Do not be misled by the expression 'the greatest' – the remaining three sonatas following the 'Hammerclavier' are no less 'great', but they displace less air and demand less comment; for sheer physical weight and enormous proportions the 'Hammerclavier' is Beethoven's most gigantic pianistic conception (except for the Diabelli Variations).

If the 'Hammerclavier' is not 100 per cent successful all along the line it deserves, perhaps for that very reason,

*The reader must turn back to Chapter 5 of this book for the answer to the question: why did Beethoven use this name? (He used it also for the Op. 101.)

volumes of analysis. This has been accorded it by many other commentators – Bülow, Busoni, Tovey and others – whose works I recommend to zealous students.

The 'Hammerclavier', then, will have to be seen as a problem. Its huge proportions, the demands it makes on the performer and the listener, the contempt with which the composer seems to treat the instrument, not caring whether the sound it produces happens to be harsh and ugly or (as is the case from time to time) beautiful and entrancing, as long as mind triumphs in the end over matter – all this puts this sonata obviously beyond the reach of any talented student, for even great and mature artists look upon it as a battle-field, and the battles are not always victorious for the artists – all too often it is Beethoven who wins. Nor is it fair to blame Beethoven's deafness for any unpleasant sound in the 'Hammerclavier', for this work is followed by the mellifluous-sounding Op. 109, surely a proof that the ugly sounds were either intentional or a matter of indifference to Beethoven, who could imagine beautiful sound even though he could not hear it.

Basically the first movement offers no great problem to analysis, only its length is unusual, and the love of contra-puntal writing is even more noticeable than in the preceding Op. 101. There is a short fugato in the development, casting forward the shadow of the 'fugue to come'. The movement ranges very freely to remote tonalities like G major or B major; it is on the whole vigorous and strong in character, even a little bellicose – the first subject flashes out like a drawn sword – and the lyrical relief of the wonderful ro-mantic second subject is but short-lived.

Perhaps this is the moment to warn the player against taking Beethoven's metronome markings too literally. There are those who accept them as sacrosanct, some glaringly obvious absurdities notwithstanding, with which view I disagree. Whether Beethoven's own metronome was faulty (as is sometimes maintained) or whether we have here just another proof that composers can be wrong about speeds, it is a far better proceeding to follow one's own natural feeling than to follow a machine. If you trust yourself to tackle a work like the 'Hammerclavier' at all, you should trust your ability of determining tempo according to your judgement. At all events, a speed arrived at in any other way, possibly *against* your natural instinct, would not make for a very convincing performance. Beethoven's metronome markings tend to be too fast. It seems a good plan to try out the indicated tempo first – do not discard anything coming from the composer without giving it a chance – but if it goes totally against the grain, drop it unhesitatingly. We know that Beethoven himself decided eventually against metronome markings, possibly because his own intentions with regard to tempo turned out to be changeable; and we performers need not impose upon ourselves more consistency in this respect than did the composer himself. My own tempo ideas have indeed undergone some changes in the course of years (albeit not very extreme ones), and this natural state of things should not unduly disquiet anyone who looks upon music-making as a function of the living, developing, changing human mind. We are entitled to change our ideas from time to time.

To return to our theme – the 'Hammerclavier' – at this point, the metronome marking of the first Allegro is rather too fast, that of the Scherzo quite reasonable (only the 'minore' section demands some slight slackening and then a sudden accelerando – this 'minore' incidentally seems at first glance homophonous but is in actual fact a canon), the marking of the wonderful slow movement is a little too fast, that of the fugue much too fast. This Adagio sostenuto in F sharp minor, one of the deepest and most moving elegies in the whole of Beethoven's work (to which he added two notes just before it went into print!), needs an interpreter who is equally endowed both intellectually and emotionally to do full justice to the expressive intensity of every turn of phrase and every harmony without disrupting the architectural unity of the sonata form. Perhaps these are commonplace words to describe something infinitely subtle, but a glance at the composition itself will convince the reader that the fulfilment of this seemingly simple requirement presents

129

quite a problem. The Adagio is very long: it accounts for nearly half the time of the whole sonata. Its demands on the player's powers of concentration are enormous: there must be no 'dead' places, and any slackening of the emotional intensity leads to the deadly danger of boredom. Nor is there any time to breathe when it is over; for the Finale starts immediately with a slow, introspective soliloquy in which Beethoven seems to try out and discard various ideas (rather on the lines of the Ninth Symphony's 'O Freunde nicht diese Töne') until, heralded by trills, the 'Fuga a tre voci' erupts. Its greatness lies, not in technical perfection such as we find in a fugue by Bach, nor in any mathematical infallibility that puts music next to science – Beethoven was no scientist nor mathematician. If I may be allowed to quote them, two passages I wrote regarding this fugue in some programme notes for a complete performance of the thirty-two sonatas still express fairly accurately what I feel about it:

If it is something less than a good fugue, it is surely also something more. The savage yet orderly rush and swell of this amazing piece certainly suggests something prehistoric and universal – the planets perhaps or the creation of the world . . . the message of the work is, on the whole, one of optimism. Does it fail in conveying its great spiritual message in sounds equally great? It would be presumptuous even to try to answer that question. At all events no artist ever aimed higher. The controversy about the purely artistic achievement the 'Hammerclavier' sonata represents will no doubt go on. The faith of the believer is not susceptible to denigrating argument, and the doubter, more often than not, will be carried off his feet by the elemental force of sheer human greatness.

Beethoven lost little time before the huge Op. 106 was followed by the more gentle Op. 109. This is a miracle of construction, especially the first movement: after just a few bars of the Allegro it seems suddenly to change course and becomes an 'Adagio espressivo' of improvisatory character – this would result in fragmentariness in any composer but Beethoven, whose technique compels the Adagio to form convincing unity with the Allegro. But it is impossible to deny that the Allegro-Adagio-Allegro-Adagio-Allegro alternation which is the shape of this movement presents problems to the interpreter. The second movement – Prestissimo – is another sonata form; it is passionate and turbulent and is frequently given too slow and sedate a performance. The crowning glory of the work is undoubtedly the last movement, a wonderful Andante with six variations. These variations differ from other sets in the sonatas in that they are highly contrasted in tempo, mood and character. The indicated changes of speed, a striking feature, make one wonder whether Beethoven intended some of his other sets of variations to be performed in this kind of style too, rather than in the strictly uniform one now known as classical. Even the eventual return of the unadorned theme – because of its epilogue character – seems to demand a somewhat slower tempo than its first statement, but only sensitive players will hear, and obey, this unspoken demand. The whole sonata, so freely and yet so firmly constructed, is also a miracle of beautiful golden piano sound – obviously the 'poor old deaf master' had this at his command when he wanted it!

The penultimate sonata, in A flat major, Op. 110, is heard fairly frequently in our concert halls and is loved by artists and public alike. It is an 'affectionate' work, seemingly at peace with the world, except for the last movement. The opening is marked 'con amabilità'; the F minor 'Allegro molto' second movement, a kind of scherzo in $\frac{2}{4}$ time, shows Beethoven in his 'unbuttoned' mood; since Bülow it is generally held that the metric meaning of the first bar is a so-called 'anacrusis', which means that the strong bar is the second one and so on throughout the piece, the ultimate proof being the coda – a view with which I agree but with which Artur Schnabel disagrees. The serenity of the sonata suffers eclipse in the last movement, which is made up of a mysterious anguished recitative, an 'Arioso dolente' and a three-part fugue; then the fugue is interrupted, an even more anguished version of the 'Arioso' returns to give way to the inversion of the fugal theme and another fugue on this; finally the fugue becomes a triumphant chorale and ends the sonata in a blaze of glory. All this is welded together to a

131

piece of compelling unity in what is one of Beethoven's greatest structures.

In the last two sonatas discussed Beethoven dispensed with the customary repeat of the exposition of the first movement. Examples of this innovation can also be found earlier on, in Op. 54, 90 and 101. But evidently he had no intention of carrying this change in the traditional sonata form into the realm of theoretical reform. He did not say, for instance, that the repeat is a mere formality – which it often is – and should be scrapped forthwith. Having carried out this particular operation in several cases, we now see him returning to the traditional form, repeat and all, in the very last sonata. Perhaps it is no accident that, when his language is at its most personal, least conventional, Beethoven uses the strictest possible form in which to say what he has to say.

The first movement of Op. 111 – yes, we have come to the last canto of our huge epic – shows no deviation from the conventional sonata form (which is preceded by a slow introduction). The second movement is a set of variations on the simplest of themes. But what depth, what plasticity in the subject matter, what compelling power and breadth in the contrapuntal elements. The contrast between the two movements could not be more pronounced: the first sombre, chaotic, passionate, the second all tranquillity, peace ('all passion spent'), with a crystalline ending of trills suggesting the starry firmament. This contrast is so striking that one well-known musician went as far as to say that there are two kinds of pianist, those who can play the first movement of Op. 111, and those who can play the second; none can play both. Be that as it may, certainly the whole sonata is musically the most taxing of the lot (excepting perhaps the 'Hammerclavier') and demands the greatest maturity from the player attempting to tackle it. It is almost as if Beethoven at the end of his life took a last glance at that life, passed its important events in review and drew some final conclusions.

As a matter of fact, Beethoven's last word in piano music was not the last piano sonata. It was followed by some beautiful sets of Bagatelles and that monumental set of thirty-three variations on a Waltz by Diabelli – if anyone needed proof that Beethoven was neither 'written out' nor 'tired' it is here in the freshness and richness of the Diabelli variations.

The Diabelli Variations

Resulting from a publicity stunt of the music publisher Diabelli, who invited distinguished composers of the day to write one variation each upon a rather worthless waltz tune of his own composition (Schubert and the boy Liszt were among the contributors) – this amazing tour-de-force of craftsmanship shows the aged Beethoven at the very peak of his powers. Not content with writing the one variation required of him, he wrote 33, amongst which is some of the most profound, most abstruse, and most complicated music ever invented for the piano. Marches, scherzi, slow movements, fugues crowd the pages of this work in unbelievable profusion, the last word being said by a heavenly tempo di menuetto, and not by the pompous double fugue immediately preceding it (a typical late Beethoven gesture!) – and all this on Diabelli's absurd little tune.

There is no doubt that these variations lack the formal unity and logical design of some of the other sets (like the 'Eroica' variations Op. 15), but who would expect these things from such an encyclopaedic summing-up of all Beethoven's pianistic dreams? Those who attempt to perform the Diabelli variations will know that by judiciously distributing pauses and by the opposite method – that of telescoping a whole group of variations into one – the work can be made to sound almost like a four-movement sonata, instead of a random selection from a chaotically fertile imagination. But this is straying into the rarefied atmosphere of the highest art of interpretation.

Practical conclusions

Perhaps a word on the interpretative and pianistic aspects.

What constitutes a Beethoven player is, of course, not nimble fingers, rapid octaves, or brilliant trills (all these things are taken for granted) but spiritual penetration of the music, sense of expression, sense of form, imagination in which the monumental whole and the carefully polished detail live peaceably together, and – above all – humanity. But it stands to reason that one must have the equipment to make the instrument do the composer's bidding. A fumbling amateurish technique, substituting 'feeling' for accuracy, wrong notes for impetuosity, will not produce good Beethoven playing, no matter how 'classical' the style in the pedantic sense of that word. Beethoven's own views on what is sometimes called 'rubato' but what I prefer to call agogic freedom will be found quoted in extenso in Chapter 14 on Chopin, and I will not waste any words on them here.

In Beethoven's piano writing the obvious tendency, compared with Mozart's or Haydn's or Clementi's, is towards greater sonority. The demands on the player's sense of balance are stringent. The easy division into right-hand melody and left-hand accompaniment is often replaced by a much more sophisticated pattern – the ear decides what component element of the total sound deserves what priority. The thin and often boring scales and figurations of earlier music are almost abolished. Beethoven, from the middle period onwards, requires thicker, heavier sound in the 'accompaniment', which is sometimes entrusted to the right-hand while the left has the melodic line above it (an example of this hand-crossing is the opening of the rondo in the 'Waldstein' Sonata). The so-called Alberti bass hardly ever appears: the 'leggiero' touch is often replaced by the 'non legato', the melody getting greater depth of touch and a broader singing tone (Beethoven had broad finger tips and used the flat finger quite a lot, according to his pupils). Pedal becomes an important factor, and should be used more often than is marked. In the late sonatas there are certain 'empty' sounds – the two hands playing at great distance from each other, at opposite ends of the keyboard – which are likely to give even artists with a highly developed sense of balance (balance of sound, of course) some hard nuts to crack. The problems are nearly always soluble but not simple. Double notes, especially thirds, require some diligent technical work in that field, and Beethoven uses them freely; chords, octaves (in glissando and other formations), prolonged staccato passages – we have here the 'modern piano technique' in all its panoply and full regalia. Schubert used the piano more mellifluously, Chopin discovered new territories – but I for one cannot admit the possibility of a fine Schubert or Chopin or Liszt player who did not go through the Beethoven school first. This is valid on the intellectual and the technical level.

Beethoven's music must be phrased amply, generously and flexibly. Punctuation – commas, full stops, colons and semi-colons – should be earnestly studied as to the exact place and time required. Beethoven's slurs, along with those of other classical composers, are not always clearly defined: one must use one's judgement to determine where they begin and end. The dynamic markings, much more carefully set than Mozart's or Haydn's but not as carefully as those of later composers, must be rigorously observed; special attention should be paid to the frequently occurring accents on single notes (fz or sf or sfz or simply >): to tone them down or to disregard them would be totally un-stylish – no intentional roughness in Beethoven should be glossed over. Another most frequently occurring marking is the so-called 'subito piano', that is to say a sudden piano preceded by a crescendo (◄ or cresc. ... p.) or by a ff or f. This is a typical Beethoven device; to make it come off properly a very slight break or comma between the end of the crescendo and the sudden piano can hardly be avoided, thus ◄'p. The same applies to the opposite: a sudden fortissimo after a diminuendo or piano. Indeed all violent dynamic contrasts demand this very slight break in the agogic continuity – and not only in Beethoven. On the other hand, do not be tempted to draw too subtle conclusions from occasionally seeing piano (p) and pianissimo (pp) used indiscriminately. It was left to later composers to distinguish consistently between these

135

notions; in Beethoven they are often interchangeable, as are forte and fortissimo. The character of the music decides.

To conclude in a more general way. There is no doubt that Beethoven, a man of the people, brought music nearer to the people, not by any concession to vulgar taste – far from it – but by somehow communicating either his very real involvement with the fate of mankind or simply his nature, the common clay he was made of. His music seems to make us feel that, all genius as he was, Beethoven was like the rest of us. The aristocratic artist Mozart created music for the select few, Beethoven for everybody, including both the select few and the non-musical. Until his time music was a fascinating and elegant game; with Beethoven it became a world force.

Fourteen
Chopin

Those before him

What makes a 'great' pianist? Surely it is not just manual skill nor the ability to invent new sound effects. The short-lived reputations of such characters as Kalkbrenner, Thalberg, Dreyschock and Steibelt rather prove this point. They flashed across the stage of pianistic virtuosity, perhaps dazzling the ignorant by something we have come to call a 'gimmick': the then new effect of distributing a melody between the two thumbs in the middle register of the instrument while above and below it was accompanied by harp-like figurations; or the sustained tremolo effect, taken from the orchestra and skilfully transferred to the pianoforte; or the effect of very rapidly repeated notes, sometimes even in octaves or chords. We can ignore them all.

Carl Czerny could at least claim to be a link between Beethoven and Liszt, being pupil of one, teacher of the other. But he is no longer remembered as the composer of large-scale works for almost every combination of instruments, fertile in many forms of art, only as a somewhat pedantic purveyor of technical exercises, recommended by some teachers and loathed by many successive generations of students who have spent years of slavery in practising them.*

J. B. Cramer is also remembered mainly for his *Études*, praised by Beethoven, but we know very little of how he played the piano.

*In my own lifetime the famous pianist Joseph Lhévinne gave a very long series of piano recitals in which he performed all Czerny's works for piano, thus making good commercial capital of his own mis-spent youth.

Muzio Clementi, Italian by birth, English by adoption, was a great musician whose piano sonatas, unjustly neglected today, must have influenced Beethoven more than historians are prepared to admit. His great work *Gradus ad Parnassum* suffered the appalling indignity of being shorn of all its musically valuable material by vandalistic editors, and published in this mutilated version as a collection of exercises, whereas it is, in fact, a microcosm of piano playing, such as Bartók attempted some two hundred years later. (More about him in the 'history' chapter of this book.)

J. N. Hummel and the Irishman John Field, employed by Clementi in his firm Collard & Collard, piano makers, were both historically important figures, for they exercised a considerable influence upon one of the greatest creative and recreative artists of the pianoforte who ever lived: Frederic Chopin. It is plain to any student that in its treatment of the instrument Hummel's Piano Concerto in A Minor has an undeniable claim to being the ancestor of Chopin's Concerto in E Minor. Elegant 'passage work', double thirds, dramatic recitative-like eloquence, richly decorated singing episodes devised to display the previously unheard-of possibilities of instrument and instrumentalist – all abound in the Hummel precursor as they do in the Chopin descendant; and even though Hummel had not Chopin's genius the period charm and pianistic richness of the Concerto in A Minor explain why Liszt played it quite often and with enjoyment.

Display; mere virtuosity? Yes, certainly. But is not every kind of performance offered to a public a display of some sort? Even the perfect rendering of a great adagio by Beethoven not only requires a high degree of virtuosity, but, by being played on a concert platform, automatically becomes a performance, and therefore display. We are too conditioned, by loosely using certain expressions in a pejorative sense, to condemning what is the purpose of all art: self-expression of the artist to the delectation of his fellow human-beings.

Hummel, then, we must recognize as one of the important stepping-stones leading to Chopin, at least in the instrumental sense.

His contemporary Field is better known as the composer of some charming works called *Nocturnes*, a word he is said to have invented, at any rate in the sense he and later Chopin used it; but his piano concerti (seven in number), though no longer performed, contain some charming music and are unjustly neglected. A heavily built Falstaffian figure, fond of drink by all acounts, he was described by contemporaries as a player of surpassing tenderness and charm – and so devoted to his art that he is said to have answered the question put to him on his death bed 'what is your religion?' by 'I am a pianist'.*
Not only was the influence of this remarkable man very noticeable on Chopin but rather surprisingly he also spent long years of his later life teaching in Russia, and Glinka, the 'father of Russian music', was his pupil. What a vast amount of unexplored conjecture opens here to the historian; what an interesting figure is revealed in this drink-sodden Irishman who put the stamp of his personality on the Pole Chopin and the Russian Glinka! By the greater force of their genius, they both surpassed him. But then, according to Leonardo da Vinci, it is a poor pupil who does not surpass his master.

Let us look back in time for a passing instant to the already dim figure of Ignatz Moscheles, a once highly successful pianist, highly thought of by Beethoven; a fertile composer of bravura études, his greatest merit seems to have been championing Beethoven's music, much to the composer's satisfaction. Schindler – Beethoven's pupil and biographer – cast the aspersion of anti-semitism on his great master ('he did not love the children of Israel'), but later musicologists found Schindler's nasty allegation untrue, and Beethoven's friendship with Moscheles seems to bear this out.

Chopin, the great pianist

So we come back to the initial question 'what makes a great pianist?' If not manual skill, nor invention of new sound effects, nor the ability to make the instrument sing, nor even self-effacing humility in the service of a great master com-

*I am indebted to Mr Frank Merrick for this information.

139

poser's thought, nor the sum total of all these necessary pre-requisites, then we are driven to the conclusion that only the pianist who is also a great *creative* genius deserves to be called a great pianist.

Beethoven's greatness transcends any one instrument, and perhaps even, in its universal humanity, transcends music herself. He is too big for this limited stage. Indeed the great creative pianist is of necessity a specialist, a self-limiting product of his own inner world. This world owes its very existence to the instrument; an entirely new world, both limited and limitless, alive with creations of the imagination inspired by the instrument and offered back to the instrument, somewhat like parents, in a perfect marriage, might offer their children to each other.

Neither Hummel nor Field belonged to that category; the comparatively slight creative gifts of these minor masters allowed them to come within a certain distance of greatness but not quite to achieve it.

Chopin, however, undoubtedly comes into this category, and in the next chapter I shall try to show why Liszt – certainly a very great pianist – was only with about half his nature a piano composer. His tendency was not to limit himself but rather to extend in all directions, while Chopin had the instinct, or the wisdom, to stay within his world, within the kingdom of which he was absolute monarch: the piano. The works he produced in which the piano shared the honours with other instruments – his chamber music and songs – though certainly not without charm and distinction add little to the glory that was Chopin the piano composer.

The concerti

Even in the two piano concerti, and one or two other works for piano and orchestra, there is a constraint, a dutiful lip-service to the rules of the game, as if the presence of the orchestra, so far from being an inspiring pair of extra wings lifting the genius of the piano to even higher flights, was rather a tiresome bit of convention to which from time to time a polite but somewhat inhibited bow had to be made. The really magical things in these works seem to happen in spite of rather than because of the orchestra. (It is of course possible that Chopin did not do the orchestration himself but entrusted it to another musician; such a theory has been put forward, and, as we shall see, Liszt had a similar problem.)

In the Concerto in E Minor – called Number One, but second in order of writing – we see Chopin at loggerheads not only with the orchestration (assuming that its author was indeed Chopin) but also with the form. He tried to reverse the traditional arrangement of keys and introduced the second subject in E major in the exposition, and in G major in the recapitulation, instead of the other way round. This did not prove very successful. The exposition is monotonous for the composer seems unable to leave the E tonality. The development makes up for this as it is prolific in modulation. But instead of returning to the original tonality the recapitulation again leads away from it. Thus the tonality is first asserted too strongly and then treated with too much reticence. The 'Romance' second movement and the dance-like Finale are charming but not profound; in the Finale one gets the impression that Chopin must have admired Weber more than a little.

The piano writing in these early works is wholly admirable; it is perhaps even more brilliant in the 'second' Concerto in F Minor. This is also shorter and better constructed, but curiously we again meet the reluctance to accept the conventional key relations as between first and second subject and between exposition and recapitulation. In this case Chopin presents his second subject in the relative major, A flat, both in the exposition and in the recapitulation, making a last-minute 'dash home' into F minor just before the end of the first movement.

It is interesting to see these early attempts to inject something new into the classical sonata form. Later, in the two great piano sonatas, Chopin saw the truth that form was something that grew out of the subject matter rather than an old bottle into which one poured new wine, and we shall see with what marvellous results.

But meanwhile I must mention the remarkable nocturne-like second movement of this Concerto in F Minor, with its extraordinary 'dramatic recitative' middle section in which the piano exclaims, sobs, thunders and whispers against a sombre orchestral background of string tremolos. The rhythmic freedom of the declamation is highly original, and cannot be explained by Chopin's well-known love of Italian opera. (This recitative device is used with even more stunning effect in the *F Minor Prelude*, from Op. 28.) The last movement of this beautiful F Minor Concerto is distinctly Polish in character: almost a mazurka, the piece is slightly melancholy and very graceful, and the intricate piano figuration gives us a glimpse of the nimbleness of the Chopin fingers.

The sonatas

In case anyone still believes in that age-old classification of Chopin as a 'miniaturist', they should make themselves acquainted with the second and third piano sonatas (the first one, a weakish product of immature if promising youth, had better be ignored), the ballades and scherzi, and the *Fantasia* in F Minor – all large-scale works, great in design, perfectly proportioned and so naturally constructed that form and content cannot be separated even by the most careful analysis. The *Barcarolle*, Op. 60, fits into no category except that of a perfect masterpiece – of indescribable eloquence, tenderness and passion.

The two great sonatas already mentioned form integral parts of every pianist's concert repertoire, and the passage of time has not damaged their audience appeal. Perhaps we tend to forget the singer and take the song too much for granted, because both have become familiar throughout decades of everyday life. So it is necessary to restate that the genius who created the Funeral March (of which, alas, the sacrilegious description 'hackneyed' has been used), and the Finale of the Sonata in B Flat Minor, which is like an Edgar Allan Poe horror story – that the genius who created all this and much more was one of the greatest the world has ever seen.

There is much to fascinate the professional musician in the formal and harmonic boldness of these sonatas (the scrapping of the traditional recapitulation of the main subject in the sonata form, the use of unison for a whole movement, which leaves the element of harmony totally obscured but yet present to the percipient ear and much else). There is a be-wildering mass of problems for the pianist. But what rich re-wards when the problems are solved!

The B Minor Sonata in particular exploits the orchestral possibilities of the piano, but remains so pianistic that no one has ever dreamed of orchestrating it; nor is such a venture to be recommended, tempting though it may seem. However the pianist is entitled to let his imagination be fired by the sound of clarinets, bassoons and horns in the middle section (Trio) of the Scherzo movement, or that of trumpets and trombones in the last movement, to name but two examples.

It is preferable, perhaps, to leave the discussion of Chopin's large-scale, but not cyclic works to where a word or two will be said about interpretation. The miniaturist Chopin, the creator of the Studies, Preludes, Mazurkas, the Waltzes, Polonaises, Nocturnes, still has to be, not indeed evaluated (for his greatness is not in doubt), but, rather, brought nearer by special pianistic searchlight, to those who wish to study his works.

Chopin, the miniaturist

If any part of Chopin's music has suffered more than another at the hands of amateurs it is surely the technically more accessible nocturnes, and some of the waltzes – those with the 'salon' flavour, entertainments, no doubt, which make no claim to any profundity and could even be called, by severe critics, 'genteel' – not that Chopin ever wrote anything in really bad taste. The fact that these waltzes, some of which are full of charm, wit and brilliance, appealed to a middlebrow Victorian bourgeoisie, should not be brought as a criminal charge against them. Nor should the nocturnes, exquisite lyrical effusions, suffer critical degradation because sentimental young ladies used them, in days long gone by, to comfort their repressed libido. Pianists who avoid works like the great waltzes in E flat, A flat and the beautifully melancholy one in A minor, or the great nocturnes in C minor, C sharp minor, F major, the long, tender one in B major (with the wonderful chain of trills and the orientally coloured ending) and many, many others, are guilty of peevish discrimination. For if these pieces are 'too sweet', or not very 'relevant' to our cheerless age, they are still expressive of another, happier age, and therefore entitled to bring pleasure to us poor deprived humans.

Like any other music, the interpretation of a 'great' Chopin nocturne depends on the taste of the player. Like a good cook, a good player will not put too much sugar into what is already full of honey; he will not labour the obvious sentiment, nor fall into the rubato trap, so tempting in some of these pieces. An expressive, tender, dynamically a little restricted style (with exceptions!) will be chosen by the good Chopinist who knows how to make the piano sing.

The *Berceuse*, one of Chopin's most inspired, tenderest nocturnes (distinguished perhaps by its innocence and the absence of eroticism), must have given rise to a contemporary and much reiterated fallacy about Chopin's rubato: the fallacy that Chopin played rubato in the melody only, keeping strict time in the accompaniment. Only in the *Berceuse* can this idea be carried out with anything approaching success; almost everywhere else it must result in the two hands not being together.

While on this subject of rubato (about which I say more later), I should mention, *en passant*, that the so-called 'Viennese lilt' cannot be recommended in the accompaniment of Chopin's waltzes. This Viennese waltz rhythm, as handed down to generations of *Musikanten* since Schubert and the Strauss family, consists in a slightly anticipated second beat. Instead of

you hear something like this

(Needless to say, this notation does not do justice to the rhythmic subtlety of Viennese or Hungarian gypsy bands but expresses in a simplified way the essence of this charming deviation from strict three-four time.) But Schubert's and the Strauss brothers' waltzes were essentially dance music, and Chopin's were drawing room music in waltz form, or, better expressed (since such a thing as 'waltz form' does not really exist), music in waltz rhythm, highly stylized at that, in which sparkling piano writing and piquant harmony are the main points of interest.

It is a mere accident if any of these pieces can be danced to – and exactly the same applies to the mazurkas. These, and to some slighter extent the polonaises, are Chopin's most nationally coloured creations, imbued with Polish fervour, a mixture of the nostalgic, the fiercely and proudly rhythmical, and that touch of French elegance in the subtle, chromatic and yet totally natural harmonic thinking, that makes them perfect in the Mozartian sense. It matters little that this very perfection and originality limits, not the universality of their appeal, but the number of pianists of other than Polish nationality who could hope to approach them with the right understanding. For 'understanding' in this case means not a function of the reason but one of the blood. I myself tend to keep away from the mazurkas, not from lack of affection but from respect for national affinities which must have the last word in this field of music. But, as I said before, this matters little for there are plenty of fine Polish artists to whom the mazurkas represent their mother tongue. So why not leave them to flower in their natural soil, rather than try to imitate the 'accent' in our clumsy foreign way?

A similar restriction, but on a slighter scale, applies to the polonaises. On a slighter scale because what is idiomatic and Polish-national is here offset by pianistic brilliance and rich sound, things which are open to pianists of any race. So a slight lapse from authenticity of style matters less in the polonaises, if skill, power, and temperament are adequate, than in the slimly-drawn mazurkas, where the chance for virtuoso arabesque or orchestral effect is almost absent. In fact the polonaise seems to be a more 'international' dance form than the mazurka, and many more polonaises were composed by non-Polish composers (there is an example by Beethoven, and even one by J. S. Bach himself!) than mazurkas. The charming mazurkas of Balakirev have a distinctly Russian flavour – very different from those of Chopin – as well as florid, Lisztian, piano writing.

But, to return to the polonaises of Chopin, surely here we have Chopin at his most un-Chopinesque. For what pianist would play them in an effeminate, dreamy, rubato style? Firmly rhythmical (by which I do not mean mechanical), and mostly masculine music, they should be performed in a heroic, aggressive, even swaggering style. A healthy exhibitionism in, for example, the famous octave passage of the *Grande Polonaise in A Flat* is not at all misplaced, for this piece should not be made to sound like a dull octave study (however efficiently played) but rather a tremendous crescendo with a crashing climax at the end. (I personally prefer to make this passage into *one single crescendo* from beginning to end, a deviation from orthodoxy of text reading. This is one of the very few passages where I allow myself, in all humility, to disagree with Chopin's dynamic markings but not of course with the actual text.)

The *Polonaise in F Sharp Minor* is a mixture of polonaise and mazurka, and the *Polonaise-Phantaisie*, perhaps the most interesting and mature work of its kind, as well as the harmonically most advanced, a mixture of polonaise and (almost) nocturne. The polonaise rhythm comes and goes, at times almost disappears, but somehow it always works its

way back to the surface, and its fusion with the tender nocturne elements is so perfect and so natural that we must admire Chopin's craftsmanship and mastery of form, sometimes questioned by critics. The piano writing is superb; especially interesting is the impressionist use of the pedal shown below.

(Some pianists use the device of silently retaking the chord and changing the pedal at the end of the passage, and this idea should not be rejected out of hand, although Chopin might have preferred the sound slightly more blurred by the inclusion of harmonically alien notes. The Steinway sostenuto pedal, combined with selective use of the 'loud' pedal, might present an alternative solution.) In the great climax of the last two pages Chopin uses a notation frequent in J. S. Bach (and Schubert) but rare in the works of romantic composers: triplets and dotted rhythms, to be played simultaneously, so that the semiquaver equals a triplet note in value. In another example of this notation, the

147

Prelude in E Major (Op. 28, No. 9), the execution is different: the semiquaver comes *after* the third triplet note. There is no valid rule – the player must use his own judgement.

The preludes

The 24 *Preludes*, Op. 28, occupy a unique place not only in Chopin's work but in all piano literature. They are more epigrammatic than anything that had been written before, as their average length is only about one and a half minutes. Written in key sequence of rising fifths – the relative minors always next to the majors – the complete cycle claims to be regarded as one single work. Nowadays, in our somewhat pedantic purist age, it is more often performed as one complete work, but in days gone by pianists used to play single pieces or small groups from the *Preludes* – a procedure not altogether to be condemned.

The rising key sequence is reminiscent of Bach's '48'; but the similarity is slight and the differences vast, the most fundamental one being that Bach, by arranging his preludes and fugues in chromatically rising sequence, wished to prove the practical usefulness of his newly invented system of tuning the piano,* while Chopin had no such theoretical aims. With him one prelude in each key was simply a *jeu d'esprit*, a charming conceit, with perhaps a slight underlying admonition to pianists to learn to 'think' in all tonalities. Liszt, in his *Transcendental Studies*, did something similar – with the accent more on technique – but he only completed half the cycle.

To say that the value of the *Preludes* is uneven is perhaps being over-critical. Not even Stendhal's epigrams are all of equal sparkle. Amongst the twenty-four preludes, one might possibly find one or two with a somewhat duller lustre – crumbs fallen from a rich table – and here and there one suspects a *faute-de-mieux* inclusion of something which just happened to be handy or for which no other use could be found. But these are isolated cases: Chopin had a highly developed self-critical faculty. Most of the preludes were

*See Chapter 4, p. 31.

written in Mallorca (which explains their descriptive character, so full of thunder, rain, howling storms, chanting monks, church bells both mournful and joyful, and their mood of desolation of the spirit), but the exceptions, those not created in that unhappy island and not touched by the same feverish heat of inspiration, do seem dull by comparison. However the best – and one should always judge by the best – is nothing short of perfection.

For the pianist there are some interesting technical problems, and in particular the remarkably wide stretches, as in Nos. 2 in A Minor, 19 in E Flat and 24 in D Minor, seem to indicate the presence of a hand with long fingers, perhaps Chopin's own. But skill can help overcome most of these difficulties. At this point, I wish to make a purely technical digression, incorporating some advice. In the *Prelude in E Flat* I find the undulating up-and-down and sideways arm movement useful: begin the upward motion on the note played by the thumb, and finish it on the little finger, as in an ordinary arpeggio.

And in No. 24 Chopin himself indicates the way to overcome the stretch difficulty: not by straining the tendons, or – even worse – by 'leaping' but by the simple device of leaving

the middle finger behind on the middle note, thus using it as a pivot.

When one considers that in this way the distance from

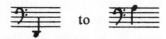

is reduced to a fifth plus an octave (which anybody can stretch), it is not too far-fetched to see the source of Chopin's inspiration in a simple technical device for the left-hand accompaniment. And the alleged resemblance of the melodic idea to Beethoven's *Appassionata* theme

can be dismissed as a mere coincidence, albeit a curious one, for Chopin was no Beethovenian.

Should you wish to give complete performances of the *Preludes* avoid long breaks, above all breaks of even length, between the short pieces, because the 'unity in diversity' intended by Chopin will thus be destroyed. Better find suitable places, after say every eight or ten, where a short pause can be made (as between movements of a sonata) with the other preludes following each other almost without interruption. My own habit is to play the first eight without pause, then make a lengthy stop, the next eight again consecutively, with a pause after the 'Raindrops' prelude, and then the rest in one long sweep, as the finale of this great sonata. This is, of course, only one possible answer to the question, how to group the preludes? There may be many other ways. That some sort of grouping is necessary, not only here but in all serially connected sets of short pieces, has become the firm conviction of one who has spent years in travelling over the keyboard.

The studies

And what of the two sets of *Études*, Op. 10 and 25? To this day they not only form the standard repertoire of every self-respecting pianist already on the concert platform, but also supply the material for daily exercise to students building their future technique. Never has there been such a perfect fusion of the athletic and the aesthetic. It is as if exercises were used to express emotion, or, conversely, emotions were expressed for the purpose of strengthening limbs, fingers and also, of course, minds; an impossible undertaking on the face of it, but how brilliantly successful!

The *E Major Study* (Op. 10, No. 3) is a love song that can move one to tears, and also an exercise in diversity of touch and double notes. The 'revolutionary' *Study in C Minor*, a despairing shout at the great national disaster that befell Poland – and what else? – also an exercise in up-and-down passage work, fortissimo, to strengthen the fingers of the left hand! The study that is sometimes called *Storm* or *Winter Wind* is a realistic nature study, a pounding melody marching on relentlessly while the wind whistles around it with macabre insistence. Can anyone doubt that here too there is the right balance between poetic theme and technical idea? The playing of chromatic tone rows is combined with the notes of the underlying harmony, the whole being a fingers-combined-with-arm exercise for the right-hand.

Many more such examples could be quoted. And where the technical idea slightly overbalances the poetic one – as in the studies in Op. 25 for double-thirds and double-sixths – the concept of 'virtuosity for its own sake' comes into its own, a concept frowned upon by severe and earnest pharisees who cannot accept the virtuoso even when he is every inch a king (as Chopin was). There must be something wrong with the understanding of a generation which rejects the idea of display. Without this idea our image of Chopin (and, of course, of Liszt too) must remain incomplete – a distorted image to suit the metabolism of those from whose needs the element of display is absent – probably only a minority.

Let us learn, through delving more deeply into the Chopin studies, that 'virtuosity' is not a dirty word.

The problem of 'unity in diversity' also applies to the studies. These pieces are not meant to be performed cyclically, but rather singly, in couples or in small groups. On the other hand Chopin made it easy for those who wish to make a 'marathon' of the complete studies, either Op. 10, Op. 25 or even both (which has indeed been done), by a very natural and musically 'comfortable' sequence of keys. It is not an uninterrupted sequence, as in the preludes, but one in which the relative minor often follows the major – sometimes the 'echelle de tierces' is substituted for the more conventional 'echelle de quintes'. A feeling of continuity can therefore be maintained, if wanted. Chopin's studies are 'all purpose' in more than one sense.

The ballades

We come now to the other large-scale works. Chopin wrote four ballades and four scherzi, all masterpieces from start to finish (Liszt contented himself with two of each – the second usually better). There are also four impromptus which are 'minor' only in length. But the number four has probably no special significance, an accident of Chopin's short but richly creative life. Several great Chopin players – Alfred Cortot amongst them – gave integral performances of the *4 Ballades*, and the *4 Scherzi* with varying success. These works, written at different periods of Chopin's life and bearing different opus numbers, encourage but do not demand integral performances, and every recitalist who tries this does so at his, or her, own risk.

The 'ballade' makes its first appearance in music with Chopin, though this form of narrative verse, usually about some sombre and tragic event, had already existed for a long time in poetry.* Whether Chopin was acquainted with the old Scottish ballades, or the German ones by Goethe, Schiller, Buerger, Heine and others, is a question for historians to decide. Chopin's source of inspiration was the Polish poet Adam Mickiewicz whose poetry, presumably for

*Not to be confused with the English 'ballad' – quite another kettle of fish.

linguistic reasons, has not penetrated into our western European consciousness.

All four ballades of Chopin, written in $\frac{6}{4}$ or $\frac{6}{8}$ time (which may or may not be a feature borrowed from the metre used by Mickiewicz) show a diversity of character, ranging from the lyrical to the dramatic, even to the sunny and gracious which, in the hands of a lesser composer, might have threatened the unity of form. But this unity is triumphantly upheld, even in the face of such a challenge as the *F Major Ballade*. This work, made of two extremely contrasting pieces (one idyllic, the other stormy), even survives the full stop at the end of the first part, and another, on an inconclusive chord, a few bars before the unexpected ending in A minor (!): only Chopin's towering genius could create perfection from so many faults. In the other three ballades Chopin does not battle with such problems of formal unity. The creative flow, strong and uninterrupted, finds its own formal solutions with unerring sureness. The form (especially in the fourth *Ballade in F Minor*) maintains links with the classical sonata, reminding us that Chopin was, in many ways, a classical composer. The two best-known ballades, in G minor and A flat major, are incontestably perfect expressions of the Romantic Age, personal in feeling and technique. Yet in their roundness and inevitability they are like natural events, and not a note could be changed, added or left out.

Chopin's remarkable instinct for economy in the use of pianistic resources is unmistakable in all four ballades: from it follows a strategically motivated tendency to save the most massive effects for the end of each piece. Thus it is on the last two pages of each ballade that the greatest effort is required of the performer. Perhaps 'effort' is the wrong word, for perfect art must be effortless. But here, in these formidable final pages, countless challenging creations of Chopin's prodigious pianistic invention – leaps, novel chord formations, double notes, octave tremolos mixed with chromaticism, and much else – are thrown at the player at breathtaking speed and with stunningly powerful effect.

Where then is the gentle dreamer Chopin, the man who

liked to hear his works performed 'mezza voce' on upright pianos? Perhaps this is one of the legends to be reduced to its true proportions, even though the composer himself seems to have been responsible for the legend.

Rubato and agogic devices

Just as we must beware of the 'Sempre mezza voce' abuse a note of warning should be sounded against the 'tempo rubato' abuse. It is lamentable how much has been sinned against the true spirit of Chopin in the name of rubato. Nor can I look with any degree of benevolence on the young reactionaries of our day; hard and dry thumping and soulless metronomic efficiency are not the answer, except perhaps as expiation of the sins committed by some of our forefathers.

Broadly speaking, the limit to which rubato can go, without resulting in waywardness and distortion, can be defined as follows: *any deviation from strict mathematical time-keeping towards flexible modification of time must remain this side of what could be expressed in terms of musical notation.* For example, to prolong quavers until they become crotchets (or dotted quavers) goes beyond the limit of legitimate rubato, and should be classed as wilful distortion. For it must be assumed that if the composer had intended minims he would not have written semi-breves. The interpreter should remember that, after all allowances are made for his idiosyncrasies and spontaneities, he is still the humble servant of the original creator. With these restrictions rubato is, and should forever be, the domain in which the recreative artist ranges freely and spontaneously; maturity of judgement and good taste, sense of style and musicianship will protect him from excesses. Above all there must be nothing premeditated about a Chopin rubato; anything planned or designed, any sign of a desire to do it 'just differently from others', is in danger of resulting in disastrous caricature.

There are other things to be learnt by the young musician

about the ways in which to handle the time element in music – sometimes called the agogic element – which should not be confused, as they frequently are, with rubato.

Rubato, then, is freedom, taken spontaneously, in the interest of intense expression, and concerns more frequently the melodic line itself. One could say that rubato lives in the *emotional* sphere of music, while so-called agogic devices originate in the *intellectual* sphere. They serve the sense rather than the feeling of music, and it is important to grasp this distinction.

These agogic devices are, broadly speaking, what punctuation is to writing: full stop, comma, colon, semi-colon. They are basically very slight, almost unnoticeable, interruptions, at times silences with the sound momentarily suspended, at other times slight additions to the regular bar, hesitations with the sound continued by the pedal. Apart from such slight interruptions, sometimes preceded by equally slight rallentando, there may be cases where the opposite measure is demanded by the music: an acceleration of the tempo, a telescopic narrowing of rhythmic values. Quite often a law of compensation operates and an acceleration is followed by a compensating broadening of the tempo, and vice versa. Thus two irregularities may add up to a satisfying regularity, and leave the listener with the feeling that the musical sense has been done justice to, while unvaried, relentless timekeeping results in an effect of mechanical dullness and boredom.

Here is an example from Chopin's Op. 35 Sonata which shows what is meant by 'comma'. The commas in brackets are not marked

by Chopin; indeed no pre-twentieth-century composer ever
marked commas. Nevertheless these are one-bar phrases, and
neither their musical sense nor the breathless character
of the whole section can be properly projected without such
commas.

And who can doubt the 'colon' in the following example
(from the Largo in Chopin's Sonata in B Minor before the
first subject opens)?

The *Prelude in C Minor* (not an 'easy piece', from the phrasing point of view) has commas, a semi-colon and a full stop,
all to be convincingly coordinated by the player.

In the G minor *Ballade* Chopin marks the long accelerando
followed by rallentando which form the connective tissue
between first and second subject. The two main melodies are
roughly in the same tempo (one should not be misled by the
'meno mosso' marking which obviously relates to the preceding quickening) but much happens in between; similar

happenings elsewhere are not always indicated in the score but left to the intelligence of the musically gifted player.

Let me repeat: what is here described does in no way belong to the 'rubato complex' to which it is often mistakenly relegated. It belongs rather to a set of auxiliary devices which enable the player to convey intellectual, structural, in short, 'craftsmanship' aspects of the work to the intellectually receptive, without didacticism.

The 'agogic accents', so-called by Riemann, belong to the same group. These are slight leans or prolongations of certain notes (with corresponding acceleration of the non-accented notes) to underline or clarify chord progressions, simple changes and complicated modulations alike. One example will be sufficient to illustrate this.

Slight lean on the notes of the left hand
marked with –

Nocturne in B

Such slight deviations from strict time frequently take place, not in the melody, but in the harmony or accompaniment. For obvious reasons these stresses are not as noticeable as the real rubato, which affects mostly the melodic element, enhancing its expressive power.

These ideas, sketchily conveyed here, may give rise to the objection: 'all very well in romantic music, but the classical style demands austere renunciation of all means not strictly demanded by the score'.

Let us hear what Beethoven had to say on the subject:

The poet writes his monologue or dialogue in a definite, continuous rhythm; but the orator, to insure that his *meaning* will be comprehended, must make pauses and rests even at points where the poet would give no indication by any kind of punctuation. In music, the performer may use the same devices as the orator ...*

In answer to the possible objection concerning the relevance or otherwise of the foregoing discussion in a book 'about the piano', may I reiterate that I deal here with rubato and agogic measures only in so far as the piano and pianists are affected by such notions. Other instruments, and groups of instruments, have their own ways of dealing with these problems. This I hope also explains the relevance of a chapter on Chopin in this book at all.

The scherzi

We come now to the great quartet of scherzi, undoubtedly amongst the most original creations of Chopin's genius, for nothing could be less like anything composed before him. The derivation of the scherzo from the old minuet – a view held by musicologists for centuries – is surely forgotten when one hears these sombre, gloomy and savage pieces, more introspective even than the ballades, more uncompromisingly pessimistic even than the great sonatas. Only an occasional friendly smile sporadically pierces the gloom for a short time – truly the very antithesis of what was understood in pre-Chopin days by 'scherzo'. Even Beethoven's scherzi, wilful and aggressive as some of them are, seem friendly, pretty creatures compared with Chopin's bitter sarcasms.

Only the No. 4 in E major is an exception, and a really celestial one at that. Here we have blue skies and gay scenes, and a beautifully and widely arched tune in a middle section that could have come out of some wistful barcarolle. The entire work, despite its repetitiveness, is so unified that I doubt if anyone ever thought of it as 'long'. It is as if the whole thing were in one long breath – breathe in at the beginning, breathe out at the end. And this is the way it should be played. The problem is not technical but artistic: how to

*From A. F. Schindler, *Beethoven as I knew him*, translation Constance S. Jolly.

sustain the piece to the end. Bars should cease to be bars, and become beats in a long bar, the groups being mostly in units of four.

Repetitiveness is the common fault of all four scherzi, and particularly Nos. 1 and 2. Whole sections are repeated note for note, and most (though not all) repeats are carefully written out, not just indicated by repeat signs, which shows the importance Chopin attached to them. They must not in any circumstances be omitted. The reason for this oddity is difficult to diagnose. Possibly the composer regarded his music as too subtle or too novel to be taken in on a first hearing, and the solution of forcing his audience to acquaint themselves thoroughly with these unfamiliar sounds by two or three repetitions may have appealed to his ironic sense of humour. And to those who are not familiar with these works none of the repeats will seem superfluous, monotonous or boring.

The *Scherzo in B Minor*, the first of the group, is a mixture of Mephistophelian concert study and gentle cradle song. This lullaby interrupts the headlong rush of the main section for a short idyllic moment. It is based on a Polish song and is embedded in almost Brahmsian piano writing

The melody should not be made into

but kept to the crotchet rhythm which corresponds to the Polish words of the song.

♩   ♩ ♩   ♩ ♩   ♩ ♩   ♩

♩ ♩ ♩ ♩ ♩ ♩ ♩ ♩ ♩ ♩ ♩ ♩

Not too many words should be wasted on the beautiful, too well-known second scherzo, which shares with the others the sardonic, introspective nature of its humour, a certain tendency towards repetition, and the rich, sonorous piano writing of the unique Chopin quality. Nor does the third scherzo need much explanation. Here an avalanche of very fast octaves gives way to a Wagnerian melody of astonishing beauty, recalling the sound of tubas, harps and all the apocalyptic orchestra of Valhalla. Here Chopin's handling of the piano comes so near to Liszt's as to be almost indistinguishable from it – a rare occurrence. This is the most concise and the shortest of the four scherzi.

The Fantasia in F Minor

Mention must be made of the *Fantasia in F Minor*, a work that once occupied the top position amongst Chopin's works in the views of contemporary musical criticism. It seems to have slipped a little from that elevated position and perhaps unjustly. But fluctuations of taste from generation to generation of music lovers are difficult to assess by absolute standards, for such standards are not at everyone's disposal.

The one obvious weakness in the structure of the *Fantasia* is the lengthy, march-like introduction, which seems rather loosely connected with the main body of the work. Indeed, it is almost detachable. However, no one has ever tried to amputate it, and it is difficult to say whether such an amputation would be a loss or a gain. The first movement of Tchaikovsky's famous Piano Concerto in B Flat Minor suffers from exactly the same structural fault: an introduction of impressive weightiness, the rightness of which in relation to the rest of the work is not proven (partly because it is never recapitulated). But far from being an obstacle, this has proved to be the main reason for the concerto's immense popularity. So let us be cautious and just state that the introduction to the F minor Fantasia is a structural fault, but is not necessarily the reason for the work's diminished popularity. The Fantasia has beautiful and original ideas. Formally it is not unlike Liszt's Sonata in B Minor in that it maintains the relationship with the sonata form (or the so-called Sonata Rondo) substituting, as Liszt does, a slow middle section for the 'development'; this beautiful slow section is partially quoted at the end of the work, thus leaving only one loose end – the introduction.

Chopin today

Ignaz Friedmann, a once famous Chopin player, said that Chopin was the man who opened, and closed, the piano. No doubt he meant that Chopin had neither ancestry nor progeny in a musical sense. One can take this statement with a grain of salt. Chopin had his pianistic precursors (Field, Hummel, Weber), and his effect on later composers, such as Liszt, Scriabin and even Debussy, was very powerful indeed. If his influence is less strong today, the reason must be that the world and its needs have changed. The genius who gave the world such unique beauty, grace and charm, and all linked with an instrument that was, until then, largely considered a percussion instrument, that genius and his wizardry are today taken entirely for granted. His works have become vehicles for young pianists to display their agility, without regard to the freshness and warmth of their poetry. There is danger in this to our civilization, and our pianistic and musical culture, and for this reason alone it is worth restating the importance of an artist who, even in his native Poland, is today treated as an export article – a product of the Nationalized Music Industry.

Fifteen
Liszt

The influence of those before him

When you look at the bewildering mass of pianistic discovery
introduced by Chopin, the floods of widely spaced arpeggios,
double thirds, sixths and octaves in every possible combination, the rich warm sonority extracted from the instrument by
an unfailing instinct for the right register; when you look at
this brave new world, made accessible to the old world by
Chopin, you wonder what was left to do by others who came
after him.

Liszt, younger by only a year, but already matured by
world-shattering success as a virtuoso, had yet much to learn
from the Polish master who stood at the beginning of his
career when the two met in Paris. For there is no doubt:
Chopin was already a master, fully formed and finished
when Liszt's more chaotic nature, still in the throes of a
romantic *Sturm und Drang*, had not yet found itself and its
way out of its predicament.

Liszt learnt much from Chopin, as he did from Paganini,
from Berlioz, from Hungarian gypsy musicians; he was
moved by Palestrina, by contemporary German, French and
Italian opera; he received inspiration from religion, art,
poetry. All this left deep traces on his musical style, so much
so that one wonders how he – *l'homme universel* – could
absorb two or three different cultures and make them
tributaries to the mighty river that was the creative artist
Liszt. Apart from his indubitable genius, the answer to the
question 'how?' lies perhaps in his beloved instrument, the
common denominator of all his diversity, this lifelong friend,
the piano.

Liszt profoundly admired Chopin (but the admiration was not mutual), wrote a book about him, and treated Chopin's pianistic achievement as his rightful heritage: he loved it, presented it to the world with incomparable virtuosity, and then proceeded further to develop it, in accordance with his own manifold and fascinating personality. He injected into the Chopin sensibility more than a drop of Paganini devilry, which brought in its wake the new effects – glissandi in thirds, sixths, octaves, fantastic arabesques right across the whole keyboard, apparently improvised without preliminary planning by a pair of incredibly gifted hands, octaves treated like single notes, and many others, beyond even Chopin's marvellous achievements. But the differences between the two masters were differences of degree rather than of kind, and it would be interesting to speculate what turn Liszt's evolution as pianist and musician would have taken if Chopin had not lived, or if their two lives had not intersected.

The Schubertian influence on Liszt was stronger than is generally assumed. You have only to look at Schubert's 'Wanderer' Fantasia to see the germs of Liszt's thematic transformation technique (see p. 171 for a discussion of this) and Liszt in fact showed his admiration for this work by arranging it brilliantly for piano and orchestra. Liszt also found inspiration in certain harmonic ideas of the great Austrian composer and his masterly piano transcriptions of Schubert songs also bear witness to his affinity with this music. This influence, already very strong, might have become even stronger and more decisive in Liszt's musical life – discounting, for the sake of argument, that of Chopin – than the influence of Berlioz or Paganini.

Would that have made Liszt a truer romantic? Probably not. For Schubert, today rightly regarded as a classical composer, second in importance only to Beethoven, might have become the spur (as in the case of Brahms) to turn the young Liszt into an anti-romantic renegade. For it is a curious fact that both the romantic revolution and the anti-romantic counter-revolution adopted the classic Beethoven as their spiritual father figure.

Replace the name Beethoven by the name Schubert, and some dim outline of what is here proposed will emerge.

In another context and in another book* I developed the view that Liszt was not a romantic composer but a futurist revolutionary; so I will restrict myself here to the above short digression, and hope that its relevance will become more obvious in time.

The question has been put: what is basically new in Liszt, as far as our central character, the pianoforte, is concerned? What has he given the world – the world of pianism, *bien entendu*, for we must accept the limitation inherent in our subject; what contribution can be simply and solely ascribed to Liszt, contribution not already made, or engendered, by Chopin?

Chopin knew what the piano could do and what it could not do, and his music – always playable if not always easy to play – grows out of its natural soil, the piano. Liszt also knew what the piano could do but rejected the idea *a priori* that there should be anything it could not do. For his faith in the power of the instrument was unlimited. If Chopin composed realistically (in the instrumental sense), then Liszt, the idealistic Utopian, bent the pianoforte to his will – as he bent music itself to his will. The surprising thing is that all the 'impossible', 'mad', 'foolhardy' piano writing of Liszt – or what seems so at first glance – turns out to be quite reasonably comfortable to the ten fingers after a little thought and practice have gone into it. Many a pianist will bear me out when I say that Chopin's piano writing – while totally piano-born and unthinkable in any other medium – does not always flow as effortlessly from the fingers as Liszt's 'transcendental' brilliance of sound.

In short, Chopin demanded from the piano only what he knew was possible, but did not always get it; Liszt demanded everything, including the seemingly impossible, and nearly always got it.

Franz Liszt: the man and his music, edited by Alan Walker, Barrie and Jenkins, 1970.

Liszt, the pianist

As in the case of Chopin the conscientious historian must refrain from any description of Liszt's piano playing, partly because no verbal effort can be expected to do it anything like justice, and partly because contemporary opinions tend to disagree and to contradict each other. Vague outlines of two opposite characters emerge: Chopin's dreamy, tender, wayward and somewhat effeminate approach contrasts with Liszt's full-blooded, passionate virility, his revelling in the display of his own diabolical gifts of virtuosity. Unfriendly critics accused Liszt of lapses of taste, while the admiring majority saw in him a near god, with unlimited power for good or evil.

A critical evaluation of all these opinions is almost impossible today. Against the accepted Chopin image stands the testimony of his own works in which the virile, the dramatic and the element of display occur every bit as often as the tenderly sentimental. And let us remember that Chopin's piano playing consisted almost exclusively of interpretations of his own works, which was not the case with Liszt – and let us further remember that the reporting ear-witnesses may have heard the sick and dying Chopin, unable to do himself justice for physical reasons. As for Liszt's piano playing, I have the testimony of a few of his pupils whom I had the good fortune of meeting in my youth: there is a measure of agreement there, to the effect that, so far from being nothing but a lion tearing into the bleeding flesh of pianos and leaving behind him bunches of broken strings, Liszt could, in fact, make the instrument sing and whisper and move his audience to tears. Above all, he could interpret Beethoven. Schindler, a somewhat pedantic disciple of the master who perhaps disagreed with Liszt's interpretations of Beethoven, was nevertheless prepared to admit that the spirituality and the fully committed personality of Liszt made even his 'un-Beethovenish' Beethoven totally convincing.

This aspect of Liszt (as well as his championship of contemporary composers like Chopin, Schumann, Balakirev, Weber, Henselt and many others) has to be mentioned in view of the still surviving criticism that his supreme mastery of the instrument was the sole source of his world success. Liszt did not, in fact, abuse his immense manual gifts but put them to the service of music.

It is not blameworthy, but praiseworthy, that the real Lisztian technique came into being when (and because) there was nothing more to be learnt, when the works of earlier masters held no more difficulties for him than the act of breathing. Liszt, admittedly stimulated by Chopin and others, set about creating a new technique, new difficulties to be overcome. We shall see presently that this was done not primarily for the sake of virtuosity as such but in the service of the highest spiritual ideals. The Liszt who practised technical exercises with the complete dedication of a monk saying his prayers was the same Liszt who, in the words of Princess Wittgenstein, 'threw his lance further into the future than anyone else'.

The studies

Twelve paperback volumes of technical exercises bear witness to the patient, single-minded toil with which Liszt created his new perfected technique. They include scales, arpeggios, octaves and all kinds of double notes as well as exercises for the 'independence of the fingers' – an idea dear to nineteenth-century teachers, as I have already explained, but less in vogue today. The exercises are useful without being in-dispensable, and are interesting to the student primarily for what they reveal of Liszt's working methods. If he really went through the whole lot every day (as I have heard it claimed) he could hardly have had time to eat and sleep. His tremendous vitality and physical strength, which lasted well into his old age, helped him as did his immense powers of concentration. (And it should be emphasized *en passant* how misguided it is for young artists to neglect these items of their equipment: good health and the ability to concentrate.)

Even after he had created his revolutionary new technique, Liszt remained faithful to his old teacher Carl Czerny, who must have found Liszt's work a complete break-away from his own method. But Czerny, who had lived all his life in the shadow of one towering genius, Beethoven, was wise enough to recognize another in his pupil Liszt and, far from trying to clip his wings (as some lesser teacher might), approved without bitterness of the pupil who surpassed his master. In return Liszt loyally dedicated to Czerny his huge *Transcendental Studies*; the dedication reads 'To Carl Czerny in gratitude and respectful friendship from his pupil' – and it is characteristic of Liszt's generous nature to remember only the good things he received from the somewhat pedantic and tyrannical Czerny, who must have caused the fiery and freedom-loving young boy much suffering. In fact, the twelve *Transcendental Studies* in their final version could not be less Czernyesque. But they exist also in a first, childishly primitive version, composed by the young Liszt in his early teens, in which the Czerny influence is unmistakable.

This is one of the most remarkable collections of studies for the piano ever created by any composer. The twelve pieces are not equal in value, quality or length. With two exceptions they have poetic titles such as 'Mazeppa', 'Feux follets' and 'Harmonies du Soir'. They are ordered in key sequence – falling fifths – and it must be assumed that Liszt originally intended a full cycle of twenty-four studies in all the keys but never completed it. In Chopin's twenty-four poetic 'genre pieces' called *Studies* one can still see traces of the technical exercise, the original purpose of the study; Liszt's studies are studies only in name, except for 'Feux follets' and 'Chasse-neige', the one being an exercise in double notes, the other in tremolos. Obviously these studies are not so much designed to develop technique as to give those who already possess it an opportunity to display their skill. Nor do these studies limit their demands on the player to mere manual skill. He must also be equal to the poetry of 'Paysage' (a little reminiscent of late Beethoven), the rich, purple sonority of 'Harmonies du Soir', the crazy rhetoric

167

of 'Mazeppa', and the bleak desolation of 'Chasse-neige'.

It is an interesting fact that between the childish first version, already mentioned, and the mature final one – in which, despite enormously enlarged proportions, the traces of the boy Liszt's Op. 1 are still quite recognizable – Liszt, already a grown man and a travelling virtuoso, composed an intermediate second version of the *Transcendental Studies*. This is of such fantastic difficulty that Busoni, no mean virtuoso himself, declared that some of these studies were totally unplayable by anyone but Liszt himself. The interesting point is that Liszt, in revising his work, simplified it, making the piano writing more transparent, more easily accessible, cleaner and clearer. The same process of simplification is characteristic of the second (or third) versions of almost all the works revised: the *Paganini Études*, some pieces of the *Années de Pèlerinage*, the first Piano Concerto and many others. That these works also gained by the revisions in unity, tension and subtlety, in economy and directness, goes without saying. Liszt's way was the way of the true artist: from chaos to clarity.

Schumann, incredibly, professed to prefer the Op. 1 of the boy Liszt to the later versions, and reproached the thirty-year-old Liszt for not yet having achieved perfect peace within – but here he revealed faulty or biased judgment, surprising in such a great and discerning critic.

Liszt used the thematic material of the 'Mazeppa' study in a later symphonic poem. Counting the childish first version, there are no less than four 'Mazeppas' in all: I prefer the one known as 'Transcendental Study No. 4'.

The *Paganini Studies* (also called 'Transcendental') are Liszt's personal homage to Paganini the composer. With the exception of 'La Campanella', which is a set of variations on a Paganini theme, these studies are in fact piano transcriptions of some of the *Caprices* composed by Paganini for unaccompanied violin. Paganini was no great composer but these pieces demonstrate the stunning virtuosity of the violinist very adequately. Liszt transcribed them very faithfully in that he avoided structural or harmonic changes, at the same time decorating these mostly poor creations with all the rich pianistic glitter which his imagination could so easily produce. The technical purposes of these studies bring them nearer to true 'studies' than the 'transcendentals': they are indeed useful exercises. In No. 1 the student can practise left- and right-hand tremolo with two or three fingers while the melodic material is allotted to another finger of the same hand. No. 2 is a study in rapid passage work distributed between the hands, with an octave study 'thrown in' as a middle section. No. 3, the well-known 'La Campanella', full of 'dangerous' leaps for both hands, makes great demands on the player with repeated notes, trills, chromatic runs and the like. No. 4, written ingeniously on one stave only but played by both hands, poses the problem of imitating the 'spiccato' effect of the violin, while No. 5 ('La Chasse') sounds almost like Scarlatti but is in fact very Paganiniesque, with its imitation of the sound of flutes and horns and the double sixths glissandi, to be executed preferably by one hand alone. No. 6 has no easily recognizable 'exercise value': it is a highly effective transcription of Paganini's own variations on a theme that later served Brahms and Rachmaninov for yet more variations. As against the Brahms work, Liszt's has the advantage of brevity and easier execution – strange as this may sound.

Transcriptions and paraphrases

It is not within the scope of this book to discuss the justification or otherwise of the 'transcription', a form of art no longer in fashion today, consisting of transferring a piece of music from one medium to another. Liszt was not the first, nor the last, to do this, but he was the one most violently attacked for doing it. Perhaps a more tolerant age is coming when it will be realized that this practice is no more criminal than that of translating literary works from one language to another.

Many of Liszt's arrangements – for example the really splendid ones of the complete Beethoven symphonies –

served the purpose of bringing the great but not yet popular or even well-known masterpieces of the eighteenth and nineteenth centuries within reach of the amateur to whom symphony concerts were not easily available. Liszt was a propagandist *par excellence*, and he made propaganda – in his own highly personal way – for all the music of which his very catholic taste approved. This included Bach's organ preludes and fugues, Schubert's songs, symphonic works of Berlioz and much else. All this falls in the category of 'arrangements', or 'transcriptions'.

Another category, that of the 'fantasy' or 'paraphrase', could also be described as propaganda. Liszt would take an opera (not necessarily a successful one) by a contemporary composer – like Wagner, Verdi or Bellini, or Gounod, Meyerbeer or Rossini – select from it two or three melodies, and weld them, not indeed into a 'potpourri', but rather into a highly organized bravura piece of virtuoso pianism, decked out in all the finery of ornamentation, figuration and variation which was at the beck and call of his ten magical fingers. These works, although making use of other composers' melodic ideas, are ultimately entirely Liszt's own. As Bartók pointed out, whatever Liszt's hand touched was first made into a pulp, and finally came out so reconstituted as to be manifestly a work of Liszt.

Obviously the musical purists will not enjoy their Mozart undergoing such treatment in the Don Giovanni *Reminiscences* – but if your mind is free of prejudice and you accept the different rules of this particular art form, you will be swept off your feet by the irresistible torrent of sound and the magisterial construction which are in fact not Mozart's but Liszt's. In this, as in other operatic fantasies, Liszt uses the form of variations. One is reminded of Busoni's argument in defence of the operatic fantasies of Liszt: if it is right and proper for any classical composer to write variations on a theme from this or that opera, by this or that composer, why is it wrong and improper when Liszt does the same thing but calls it *Reminiscences*, or *Paraphrase*, or *Fantasia*?

The Sonata in B Minor

Amongst Liszt's 'original' works, other than studies, the place of honour undoubtedly goes to the great Sonata in B minor. This is not only one of Liszt's greatest achievements, but in my opinion also one of the highest pinnacles of nineteenth-century piano music. It needs no introduction here for it is much performed on our concert platforms. Like the symphonic poems and the concerti it is in one continuous movement, in which the elements of an immensely enlarged sonata form are clearly recognizable, and in this you cannot fail to notice the affinity with Schubert's 'Wanderer' Fantasia. This affinity exists not only in the one-movement form but also, as I have already pointed out, in the thematic transformation technique – a technique in which almost everything derives from a germ theme stated at the opening. This, and the love of enharmonic modulation (about which more below), Liszt has in common with Schubert. But what distinguishes the Liszt Sonata from its Schubertian prototype, apart from its superior handling of the instrument, is the subjective 'tone': we can hardly imagine a more spontaneous outpouring, a truer self-portrait than the one Liszt has given here. We know that Goethe's *Faust* occupied his thoughts all his life, almost to the point of obsession, and the three principal characters – Faust, Marguerite and Mephistopheles (all integral parts of Liszt's own character!) are vividly portrayed. It is true that Liszt never said it in so many words, but it seems to me nevertheless that this is a 'Faust' sonata, no less so than the later symphony is a 'Faust' symphony. It goes without saying that this great and profound work should not be tackled by pianists who have no other credentials besides 'technique'. Very fast octaves, glittering passage work, vast chordal climaxes – all this must be incidental to the tortured brooding of Faust, the purity and innocence of Marguerite, the elegant maliciousness of Mephistopheles.

Here, if I may be allowed a digression, I would like to expand on the subject of enharmonic modulation, one of the many

171

bridges connecting Liszt with Schubert.

Let me first of all give a short explanation of what is meant by the expression (a rudimentary knowledge of harmony is assumed). Take the following chord:

If you identify this as the dominant seventh of D flat major, it will tend to be resolved thus:

But then substitute F sharp for G flat:

This sounds exactly the same, but the chord clearly belongs to the tonality of C minor, or C major, and its natural sequel will be this:

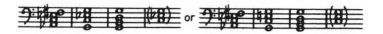

The interesting point of all this – and one that to my knowledge has not as yet received attention – is that the device of enharmonic change is essentially a pianistic, or at least a keyboard, device. Anyone who plays a string instrument (or who has paid attention to relevant passages in this book) knows that C sharp and D flat are not the same note. But on the piano and other keyboard instruments they are. Perhaps it is not too far-fetched to say that the great piano composers after Beethoven – Schubert first, then Liszt and Chopin – made use of this 'discovery' *because* they were piano composers.

Someone might object that enharmonic change, modulation based on that idea, all sounds a cerebral game, an intellectual subtlety, far from the heart of music. Maybe – but is this 'game' not based on something really quite physical: the ear, and the fingers in contact with the key?

I hope to have established, by this digression, the Schubert-Liszt affinity, hitherto neglected.

The works with orchestra

A word must be said of Liszt's works with orchestra. They include two concerti, the *Totentanz* (a paraphrase on the 'Dies Irae' melody, basically in the form of variations), *Malediction* for piano with string orchestra, *Hungarian Fantasia*, a revised and orchestrated version of Hungarian Rhapsody No. 14, a fantasy on Beethoven's *Ruins of Athens*, and the extremely workmanlike transcription for piano and orchestra of Schubert's 'Wanderer' *Fantasia*, already mentioned. There is also an orchestrated version of the two-piano 'Concerto Pathétique', recast as a concerto for one piano with orchestra (the orchestration possibly not by Liszt), and a Fantasia on *Lélio* by Berlioz, as yet unpublished. We can neglect the two last-named works, and the *Ruins of Athens*.

But *Malediction*, although an early work, should not be neglected by pianists for all the obvious signs of immaturity. These are offset by glimpses into the future, glimpses of astonishing promise – like the very opening.

Liszt was at that time diffident as to his technique of handling a full orchestra (a technique of which he was later to become sovereign master) which was presumably why he used a modest

173

string orchestra for this violent piece of *Sturm und Drang*. The piano writing is, in fact, so explosive that the string accompaniment is often unable to hold the balance; nor are the strings given a chance to fulfil their natural function – to sing – for this is too often made the prerogative of the solo piano. Nevertheless there are moments of great beauty of sound. To the student of Liszt's symphonic works it is a point of special interest that an important motive of the 'Faust' Symphony appears here for the first time.

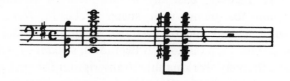

The two concerti belong to Liszt's period of maturity, his style settled and clarified, his orchestration masterly (he no longer felt obliged to let his pupil Joachim Raff help him in this respect), the piano writing brilliant yet economical. Liszt found in his concerti the final and ideal form in which to express himself: the one-movement form which comprises a variety of moods and speeds, all derived from one or two germ ideas, the transformation technique I have already discussed in connection with the Sonata in B Minor (see p. 171), and which Schubert used in his 'Wanderer' Fantasia. Liszt continued to develop this transformation technique throughout his life, but Schubert's experiment in this form remained unique. He never repeated it. Whether he would have done so had he lived another twenty years remains one of the many unanswerable questions regarding the life of that enigmatic master.

But it is not only the form that gives Liszt's concerti their symphonic character; the orchestra is lifted out of its subordinate role as accompanist, to which it had been relegated by Chopin, who took as his model the old-fashioned Hummel–Field–Weber type of concerto. Liszt divides his material impartially between the solo piano and the orchestra. In this respect his way is a return to the classics, to Mozart and Beethoven; except the orchestra is not treated in the chamber music style of the classics, but in the modern style, massive and sonorous, of Berlioz and Wagner. There are piquant and charming effects, like the triangle entry in the E flat major Concerto's third movement, where the piano's octaves, too, are treated coloristically.

The *Totentanz*, arguably Liszt's best work in this medium of piano and orchestra, is a sombre, impressive, infinitely serious study in dark colour, symphonic in structure, and uncompromisingly pessimistic in utterance. Only for a very few bars does Liszt allow a major key (the key of B major) slightly to relieve the tension, otherwise the doric mode – or D minor – predominates throughout.* It is interesting that Bartók, who loved the work, took exception to the few bars in B major just mentioned: they seemed to him too sweet, too scented, to harmonize with the rest. It is possible, however, to disagree with this judgement, and to see the working of a sophisticated artistic instinct in Liszt, who felt the need to inject, even if only for a few seconds, a drop of sweetness into the strenuously macabre which is the basic element of the composition. Contrapuntal devices, like fugue and canon, are used with dramatic effect. Of instrumental felicities only two shall be mentioned here: the repeated notes of the piano in the fugato which seem to imitate the noise of dancing skeletons, and the one and only appearance in the score of the tom-tom, just a few bars before the end. This instrument, starting very softly, makes a deafening, terrifying crescendo, eventually drowning in its noise piano and orchestra alike. If directed by an understanding conductor this should give the effect of the earth opening and swallowing the whole ghostly scene, a highly romantic notion! To those who affect a distaste for the macabre because of its romantic implications I recommend

*This statement is not strictly accurate. The key of B major does, in fact, make another short appearance in the fugato variation, and there is a brief episode in F sharp major in one of the piano cadenzas. The basic facts, however, minus non-essential exceptions, are correctly stated.

Liszt's *Totentanz* – one of his most deeply moving creations as well as one of his most prophetic and least sentimental ones.

The Hungarian Rhapsodies

For many years the *Hungarian Rhapsodies* were Liszt's best known, most often performed works, and the real popularity attained by some of them provoked an understandable counter-reaction from serious-minded musicians. We can today afford a balanced and tolerant view of these pieces, in the light of what they set out to be.

Fifteen floridly-written pieces (to which four or five more, less florid, were added by the old Liszt, many years later), the rhapsodies are based on what Liszt believed to be Hungarian folk melodies. This belief was later disproved by Bartók and other researchers: Liszt's sources were only partly genuine, some tunes were real folk-songs which had been put through a stylistic process unfavourable to their purity by the gypsies (Liszt loved gypsies, wrote a book about them and their music, but he was no scientist, and his theory identifying gypsy music with Hungarian folk music was inaccurate), and some tunes were simply works of living and known composers of the lighter kind. But be that as it may, it matters little from what sources the original melodies of the *Hungarian Rhapsodies* came; under the mighty hands of Liszt they became Liszt and nothing else but Liszt. Basically, although obviously meant to be performed separately or in small numbers, the fifteen *Hungarian Rhapsodies* constitute one vast work, a monument to Liszt's patriotism, his love for and pride in the fiery and freedom-loving Hungarian people.

The piano writing is as original as the choice of material: the piano frequently has to sound like a gypsy 'cimbalom', or a clarinet perhaps whose role in the band is to make rings of fast and shrill variations around a slow-moving tune. This is known in the gypsy world as 'explaining'.

Later trends

In the *Années de Pèlerinage* we see Liszt preoccupied with nature ('Suisse'), art (*Italie*), and religion ('Troisième Année') – in the *Harmonies poétiques et religieuses* (after Lamartine) his preoccupation is with religion alone. All these works show his gradual alienation from the Romantic Movement and his slow but sure progress into the New Age. Ultimately harmonic experiment took the place of pianistic brilliance, all florid writing disappeared. Some of the late piano pieces consist of just a few immensely significant notes, stark and austere like Bartók's bare-bones stuff, the stuff some of our twentieth-century music is made of.

Conclusions

It is rather dangerous to talk about progress in art, for art does not, in fact, progress, any more than gold or precious stones. These things are there, in the collective mind of humanity, or in the bowels of the earth, for ever waiting to be discovered, mined and used by succeeding generations of human beings, in accordance with their changing, but not necessarily progressing, needs. No one would seriously maintain that dramatic art has made progress since the old Greek dramatists, or that greater music is written today than in the time of Palestrina. Marcel Proust, somewhere in the vastnesses of *À la recherche du temps perdu*, expresses a somewhat similar thought.

Technique, however, and science, do make progress. Since early man discovered that by rubbing two bits of wood together he could make a near-musical sound (as well as a fire), we have learnt quite a lot about the mysterious universe. To put into the proper sequence all that is relevant of these mysteries, or to discover by thought processes how seemingly unrelated facts can relate to one another: that is what we call Science. To put our new understanding to practical use, to the service of Life, or of Art, that is Technique. In both these progress *is* possible because human intelligence, in its ultimately successful quest for understanding, starts at zero point.

Art does not progress, but the artist does. Liszt's progress took him straight into the twentieth century.

The somewhat glib distinction, current nowadays, between artists who are perfectionists and those who are not must be rejected as misleading. Surely every artist aims at perfection, and every artist, surely, falls short of this ideal, human frailty being forever at war with artistic intention. But I have never yet seen or heard of an artist, creative or recreative, whose endeavour was to be imperfect.

It is possible to say that human frailty made Liszt lose more battles in the fight for the highest achievement than it did in the case of Chopin, not to mention Mozart or Bach. His fiery temperament, the feverish drive of his sometimes unselective inventiveness, frequently got the better of his critical faculty. But then, what great composer was without faults? And since when is creative genius supposed to go hand-in-hand with good taste? It is typical of the injustice with which contemporary criticism treated Liszt (an injustice still to be encountered even in our current present day) that he was castigated mercilessly for faults which were condoned in other composers of his time, such as Weber, Brahms, and, a little later, Richard Strauss and Mahler. A reason for this injustice may be that Liszt's faults are on the surface, obvious to everyone, while the positive proof of his genius often lies hidden below. Beethoven also had his faults, but it takes a sharp critical mind to find them, while the greatness must be obvious to all.

And so any piece of writing concerning Liszt the composer, or Liszt the pianist, or simply Liszt the most powerful musical figure of his time, automatically becomes a Speech for the Defence, or for the Prosecution – the common fate of controversial musicians.

It has been asked whether Liszt would have been a greater, more profound composer had his gift for pianistic virtuosity not lured him to easy and shallow success. But we can reverse the question and ask whether the world of pianism suffered a grievous loss when he set aside his life of triumph, embracing an ascetic discipline as a composer. Critics of the composer (less numerous today than they used to be) answer yes to the second question, while admirers maintain that what stood between him and ultimate greatness was not lack of genius, but the glittering career achieved by his ten marvellous fingers – a career which continued to tempt him almost all his life, despite all the good advice given him by Marie d'Agoult and Princess Wittgenstein.

The conflict in an artist equally gifted in two directions – for Liszt the faculty to create and the power to interpret – is a very real conflict, the solution of which must depend on character. Perhaps Liszt had in his character an element of weakness or vanity which made him unable to resist the temptation of worldly success. But who can blame him? When the final accounts are made and all the weaknesses diagnosed and explained, there is still enough greatness left for future generations to admire – enough to enrich the lives of those for whom music represents spiritual value. The man Liszt, with all his weaknesses, was great, warm-hearted, generous to other musicians. The artist Liszt, with *his* weaknesses, put his stamp on several generations of composers – his influence is alive today.

Rossini, in one of his characteristically humorous 'Péchés de Vieillesse' piano pieces, describes himself making his last trip – to the Gates of Heaven – armed with credentials in the form of tunes from his most delightful operas. He demands admission on the strength of these melodies, but St Peter, unimpressed, refuses him entry; whereupon he happily and cynically makes his way to 'the other place'. One fears that Liszt would not join him there. The composer of the B minor Sonata, the 'Faust' Symphony, the Christus oratorio, whose sins did not include cynicism, would almost certainly be successful in seeking admission to Heaven.

Sixteen
... And After

The inevitable period of uncreative stagnation which followed the exuberance of the Lisztian proliferation era, was none the less remarkably fertile with fine pianists, some of them pupils of Liszt. Artists like Rosenthal, Pachmann, Emil von Sauer, Eugen d'Albert and many others inundated European and American concert platforms. The piano recital – introduced by Liszt – became the order of the day: the pianist who could not fill a whole evening's programme with a selection of works by classical, romantic and contemporary composers was not worth his salt. Unfortunately the compositions of Emil von Sauer and Eugen d'Albert (who composed operas in the Italian 'verismo' style which contradicted his pianistic preference for Beethoven and Schubert in a puzzling sort of way) did not survive the passage of time – but many remember, even today, their recitals and the joy their playing used to give.*

But here we must pause for a moment and remember two great pianists from Russia who were contemporaries of Liszt, the brothers Anton and Nicholas Rubinstein. Anton made a world success comparable with Liszt's, while Nicholas was immensely admired and respected in Russia, a country which, for some reason, he seems but rarely to have left. Both brothers were famous teachers (one of the most successful of our contemporary pianists, Josef Hofmann, was Anton Rubinstein's pupil), and Anton's reputation as a composer was for a time undeservedly high. His Piano

*Those who will miss some exalted names in this short sketch are reminded that the scope of it is limited to 'great pianists and piano composers'.

Concerto in D Minor and one or two of his concert studies are still performed occasionally, although they do not on the whole show much originality or distinction. Those who heard Anton Rubinstein play have left behind glowing accounts of his massive, romantic style, beautiful tone and tremendous temperament which at times carried him to waywardness and inaccuracy. Nothing has come down about Nicholas and his piano playing, nothing, that is, beyond what has become pianistic tradition in Russia, known in detail only to specialists. His 'brush' with Tschaikovsky over his negative reaction to the latter's (now so famous) Concerto in B Flat Minor is, of course, well-known.

The Rubinsteins had little sympathy for Liszt and his music. They were also on strained terms with 'The Five' (Balakirev, Borodin, Rimsky-Korsakov, Cui, Mussorgsky), the well-known Moscow-based group of composers who were both nationalist and Lisztian, and through whom Liszt exercised greater influence on Russian contemporary music than perhaps any other non-Russian musician, except John Field, the teacher of Glinka.

The Lisztian influence is particularly strong in the piano works of Balakirev, and of his friend and pupil Liapunov. It is not surprising that Liszt reciprocated this sympathy, and that Balakirev's beautiful oriental fantasy *Islamey* became one of Liszt's favourite 'battle horses'. It is a great pity that so much of Balakirev's piano music (rich, sonorous, original and sensitive and extremely well written for the instrument) is today neglected and almost forgotten even by Russian pianists, who ought to remember this important father figure of all Russian music.

As for Serge Liapunov, he was another fine composer of piano music, no longer remembered. His outstanding achievement was a set of twelve *Transcendental Studies*. Beginning with the key of F sharp major (where the Liszt set left off), it continues the Liszt sequence of falling fifths, and completes the cycle of twenty-four tonalities. The whole work is dedicated 'to the memory of Franz Liszt', the last piece being an 'Elegy for Franz Liszt' in E minor, written very much in the style of a Hungarian Rhapsody. Liapunov, in one of his letters, complained naïvely and touchingly that he could not get away from Liszt, that all he composed came out like a piece by Liszt! In this he was too modest. At least in these full-blooded, brilliant *Études* he composed music that was very Russian, very original, and Lisztian only in terms of pianistic workmanship.

No account of Russian post-Lisztian pianism can be complete without the names of Scriabin and Rachmaninov. Scriabin made the greatest impact, perhaps, on musicians, Rachmaninov on the public. Scriabin's early work was mostly Chopin-influenced, but will nevertheless interest pianists because of its technical accomplishment and elegance. His later development took him into regions of astonishingly daring experimentalism: he explored atonal possibilities – perhaps not uninfluenced in this by Liszt's experiments in that direction – and had the greatest possible effect on present-day Russian composers, even Stravinsky, and on Polish composers such as Szymanowsky.

His contemporary Rachmaninov, a pianistic world success of the Rubinstein type, was a more conservative composer than Scriabin, and his considerable output of still very popular piano music shows the influence of Liszt and Tschaikovsky as well as that of the nationalist composers. His immensely accomplished piano playing was an unforgettable experience for all who had the good fortune of hearing him in concert; he was a spellbinder and a great master.

Almost all the composers here mentioned were also great pianists. Now we must consider a great pianist, perhaps the most influential after Liszt, but whose creative work, albeit sincere and serious, is open to doubt as to its intrinsic value: Ferruccio Busoni. In many respects he recalls the Lisztian image – generous, enthusiastic, cosmopolitan, capable of sensational public impact, conscious of his high vocation as a great artist and the duties and responsibilities that implies. Busoni, like Liszt, believed that it was his duty to serve the cause of

contemporary music, and he gave perhaps the earliest performances of works of Bartók, Schoenberg and others.
He also became an enthusiastic champion of Liszt, whom he
revered next to Bach and Mozart. His piano playing, to
judge by competent witnesses, was of a sculptural, or architectural grandeur never before experienced, a virtuosity so
completely controlled that its existence was noticed only by
the astonishing plasticity and clarity with which the music
emerged – but also of a certain frigidity in the emotional
sphere.

He was, like Liszt, a great teacher, and some of his pupils
made successful concert careers, Egon Petri and Michael
Zadora in particular.

Also like Liszt, Busoni composed a few real masterpieces
in the art of transcription (Bach's *Chaconne* for unaccompanied violin, transcribed for piano, is an outstanding
example). As a composer he had many fervent champions,
but so far his place in the Pantheon of great composers seems
far from assured. Perhaps the intellectuality and coldness
that certain critically inclined listeners found in his piano
playing also prevented him evolving a really original style
of his own in his compositions. They seem to be lacking in
spontaneity of expression and it is sometimes difficult to say
what, behind the many stylistic masks he wears, the real face of
the man Busoni is like.

If Busoni was criticized for lack of emotional warmth, there
certainly was no cause for such a complaint in the case of
Paderewski, the beautiful Polish piano lion, who, red-
haired and Swinburne-ish looking, conquered all Europe
and America with his fiery, emotional virtuosity, and conquered them by storm. Highly-strung and a sufferer from
'concert nerves', his performance was apt to oscillate
between extremes of good and bad. But he had the magic
quality that hypnotizes audiences – Paderewski was simply
loved by the public, wrong notes and all. In this, and other
things, he was in the direct line of succession from Liszt.

But unfortunately, together with von Sauer and D'Albert,

Part Three: The Great Pianoforte Composers

Paderewski qualifies as a great pianist hopelessly in love with composition. To remember him as a great musician it is necessary to forget about his works.

Two significant composers of our age must make a brief appearance on these pages: Claude Debussy and Maurice Ravel. Neither one nor the other – and linking them together in our consciousness may be a popular fallacy engendered by critical carelessness – was an executant pianist. Nevertheless, their joint impact on modern pianism was far-reaching.

The label given to these composers – that of impressionism – has fortunately, together with other labels and other 'isms', faded into oblivion. This label, borrowed from pictorial art, denotes a somewhat different way of experiencing reality through the artist's perception – a way where colour, light and sensitive reproduction of atmosphere and inner meaning play a greater part than objective photographic likeness, which is rejected on the grounds that it is, in a profounder sense, quite unlike the reality it attempts to depict. This, when transferred to the field of music, does not really make much sense, because music does not attempt to depict anything, being concerned with expression, not with description of any reality outside itself. On a superficial plane, however, there are points where pictorial impressionism and its musical counterpart, as represented by Debussy and Ravel, intersect. The stress is on colour, if we look upon harmony and instrumental sound as colour, rather than line, if we substitute for line the notion of melody. Harmony, subtle, flexible, infinitely expressive and carried to the limits of what is still intelligible in terms of tonality, becomes the composer's main preoccupation, the melodic line (the 'themes' in the older music) is sometimes allowed to suffocate in all this colour, or it appears in short melodic fragments, where the older music demanded clear-cut melody. 'Tunes' are, of course, by no means absent in Debussy, and Ravel's famous *Ondine* consists of one long drawn-out, very beautiful melodic chant, around which the watery, silvery sound of the figuration splashes, gurgles and thunders in a super-Lisztian

184

fashion – but *Ondine* is the exception, not the rule. Debussy, in his different way, is deflected from 'impressionism' in the enchanting 'Children's Corner' suite; here the writing is 'linear', almost Mozartian, in its simplicity and tunefulness. In most of Debussy's piano music – and it must be stressed that works like the two volumes of *Preludes* (twelve pieces each but, unlike Chopin's twenty-four, not following any order of tonality), *Images, L'Isle joyeuse* and others ought to be in every self-respecting pianist's standard repertoire – the harmonic interest is greater than the purely pianistic one. Only in the *12 Études* is Debussy seen deliberately setting out to give pianists some hard nuts to crack. It must be admitted that in double thirds, sixths and octaves Chopin's contributions are of greater musical and pianistic value; but in the study in fourths and the one 'Pour les sonorités opposées' Debussy breaks new ground. If Debussy may be said to be more interested in harmony than in piano writing, with Ravel (who did not go much beyond Debussy harmonically) the opposite is the case: here we have piano writing in the line of succession from Liszt and Balakirev, piano writing so sculptured and precise, so sure of effect, that one marvels at the perfect craftsmanship of a piano composer who was not himself much of a pianist. Ravel brought this same precise craftsmanship to all other instruments or combinations of instruments he wrote for, which is why malevolent critics said that he composed as a watchmaker puts together a fine timepiece. But his infinite patience and attention to detail are susceptible of a more sympathetic explanation: such patience, such attentiveness could be akin to genius.

Debussy needs an interpreter of refinement and one who has at his disposal a great variety of dynamic shades in the piano–pianissimo direction. Ravel must be played very differently: with virtuosity, fire, elegance – very much like Liszt. Dynamically, no holes are barred. Ravel's old-fashioned use of Lisztian devices, like glissandi in thirds, fourths (in *Alborada del Gracioso*, for instance) and on white and black keys simultaneously, shows clearly the impact Liszt made on the twentieth century.

But it must be mentioned, *en passant*, that glissando (particularly in octaves) does not constitute a very realistic device of piano writing, demanding, as it does, not only certain qualities in the player's physical aptitude, but also a loose, easy piano action: such pianists and such pianos are both rare today.

Ravel's piano music represents the end of an era – an era opened by Debussy but which was made possible by the innovations of Liszt. The rich and heroic tends to be superseded (in later twentieth-century piano composers like Bartók) by the lean and bony. Abstract music happens to be written for piano almost by accident. Whether this development – due perhaps to a growing influence of Bach on our age – is one to be rejoiced in or deplored is a problem for future generations to discuss.

In Liszt's native Hungary there was no Liszt cult or tradition in the period immediately following his death. Hungarian musical culture, lying fallow under German domination, produced Ernst von Dohnányi, a typical figure of the turn of the century. Though splendidly gifted as a composer, he never quite freed himself from the Brahms–Strauss influence. He was a great musician and a great pianist, mostly in German classical music. His performances of certain works of Beethoven (such as the Concerto in G Major) and Schubert (the Sonata in G Major) were revelations, and helped a whole generation of Hungarian musicians find their souls.

And it was not until they had found their souls and broken away from German tutelage that a real cult of Liszt started. Undoubtedly the beginning of this is linked with the name of Béla Bartók, one of this century's foremost composers. No mean pianist himself, Bartók used his authority amongst the younger generation to spread the gospel of Liszt's music – by performing it, lecturing about it, by shifting the stress from the brilliant showiness of Liszt's piano writing to the serious, profound (and almost unknown) Liszt of the '*Weinen, Klagen . . .*' variations and the *Totentanz*. In this he went beyond even Busoni, who, exhilarated by his own instrumental mastery, was not above displaying his fireworks to a dazzled audience in operatic fantasias and the like, perhaps to the point of neglecting the more serious Liszt a little. Bartók was not interested in display of any kind but liked to underline the revolutionary harmonist in his Liszt interpretations. Being himself an iconoclast, Bartók did this most persuasively.

Perhaps if the three personalities of Bartók, Busoni and Rachmaninov could be successfully mixed in one pianist, one would have the ideal interpreter of Liszt in all his aspects.

Bartók's own piano music, still violently reacted to, in positive or negative ways according to personal conviction or prejudice, is controversial, but indubitably relevant to our age. However, to discuss the work of Bartók, or any other half-dozen composers who have contributed significantly to the repertoire of the piano in this century, would demand a volume twice the size of the present one, and in any case does not truly belong either within the scope or within the aim of this series.

Epilogue

Where do we go from here? Have we come to the end of the road, or are we going to see further glorious development in the history of the piano and piano playing?

There is a fine young generation of pianists. There is, too, a highly developed art of teaching the piano. Technique is no longer explored by trial and error, nor experience gained by making mistakes. Highly trained practitioners, imbued with the right principles reached by generations of patient workers, direct the efforts of the young in the technical field, also laying down the law with unshakeable conviction on matters of interpretation. We seem to know all the answers.

Is there, perhaps, an element of monotony in all this perfection? Has the gramophone record, the uniformity of minds, young and old, stultified the individual approach, have we lost the personal touch? Has competition ruined our souls?

Raising doubts is not what an author should do at the end of a book – he should leave that to the critics of the daily press. I have put the questions, but I dare not answer them; I will leave the answers to those qualified to judge the past and see the future.

Some selected further reading

Schumann Piano Music, by Joan Chissell (B.B.C. Music Guides, 1967).

Debussy Piano Music, by Frank Dawes (B.B.C. Music Guides, 1969).

A Companion to Mozart's Piano Concertos, by Arthur Hutchings (Oxford University Press, 1950).

Beethoven Piano Sonatas, by Denis Matthews (B.B.C. Music Guides, 1968).

Schubert Piano Sonatas, by Philip Radcliffe (B.B.C. Music Guides, 1968).

Classical Style: Haydn, Mozart, Beethoven, by Charles Rosen (Faber, 1971; paperback, 1973).

Music of Liszt, by Humphrey Searle (Dover, 1967).

Life and Music of Béla Bartók, by Halsey Stevens (Oxford University Press, 1965; paperback, 1968).

The Pianoforte, by W. L. Sumner (Macdonald and Jane's, 1971).

Frederic Chopin, edited by Alan Walker (Barrie and Jenkins, 1966).

Discography

Some Selected Piano Records

Any short list of records must necessarily be highly selective. Moreover any selection is governed by the availability of records at any given time. Nearly but not all of the records listed here were available at the time of going to press; some will no doubt disappear from circulation; others that have disappeared will, one hopes, return on other labels. The list has glaring omissions but it is designed to give the reader starting to collect records some rough guidance in starting to build up a library of piano records for himself. (R.L.)

Part One

ALBENIZ, Isaac (1860–1909) *Spain*
Iberia (complete)
Cantos de Espana
Navarra
Alicia de Larrocha
   (1973) Decca SXL6586–7

ALKAN, Charles Morhange
(1813–88) *France*
Concerto for solo piano, Op. 39
Ronald Smith
   (1970) HMV HQS1204
*Six Preludes, Op. 31; Barcarolle
Op. 65; Le Festin d'Esope, Op. 39;
Seven Esquisses, Op. 63; Two
Capriccii Op. 50; Allegro barbaro
Op. 35.*
Ronald Smith (on Schneider
fortepiano 1851, Vienna Erard,
pianoforte 1855, London) (1969)
Oryx 1803

BACH Johann Sebastian
(1685–1750) *Germany*
*Das Wohltemperierte Klavier,
BWV 846–93*
Rosalyn Tureck
   (1955) Brunswick AXTL1036–41
Maurice Cole (1962) Saga 5131–6
Glenn Gould (Bk. I)
   (1974) CBS77225
Goldberg Variations, BWV988
Rosalyn Tureck
   (1958) HMV ALP1548–9
Glenn Gould (1958) CBS72692
Charles Rosen (1969) CBS77309
Wilhelm Kempff (1971) DG139445
Partitas BWV825–30
1 in B flat: Dinu Lipatti
   HQM1210 from LX8744–5
1 in B flat
2 in C minor Rosalyn Tureck
     HMV ALP1645

191

Piano

3 in A minor
6 in E minor Rosalyn Tureck
　　　　　　HMV ALP1692
4 in D, 5 in G Rosalyn Tureck
　　　　　　HMV ALP1714

BALAKIREV, Mily (1837–1910)
Russia
Piano Sonata in B flat minor
Ronald Smith　　HMV HQS1259
Islamey
Simon Barer　　　HMV DB2675
Cziffra　　　　　HMV ALP1718
Katchen　　　　　Decca SXL2076

BARBER, Samuel (1910–) *U.S.A.*
Sonata
Horowitz　　　　　RCA RB6555
Cliburn　　　　　RCA LSB4095

BARTÓK, Béla (1881–1945)
Hungary
For Children
(Excerpts) Bartók
　　　　　　Turnabout TV4159
Mikrokosmos
(Excerpts) Stephen Bishop
　　　　　　Philips 6500 013

BEETHOVEN, Ludwig van
(1770–1827) *Germany*
Piano Sonatas 1–32 cpte
Schnabel　　　HMV COLH51–63
Kempff　　　　　DG2721 060
Sonata in F, Op. 10, No. 2
Barenboim　　　HMV HQS1152
Gilels　　　　　DG2530 406
Sonata in D, Op. 10, No. 3
Brendel　　　　Philips 6500 417
Ashkenazy　　　Decca SXL6603
Sonata in C minor, Op. 13
(*Pathétique*)
Brendel　　　Turnabout TV34122S
Rubinstein　　　RCA SB6537
Sonata in C sharp minor
(*Moonlight*) *Op. 27, No. 1*
Gilels　　　　　HMV ASD2544
Brendel　　　　Philips 6500 417
Sonata in D minor, Op. 31, No. 2
Solomon　　　　HMV ALP1303
Richter　　　　HMV ASD450
Sonata in C, Op. 53 (*Waldstein*)
Gilels　　　　　DG2530 253
Solomon　　　　HMV HQM1077
Sonata in F minor, Appassionata
Op. 57
Richter　　　　RCA VICS1427
Brendel　　　　Philips 6500 138
Gilels　　　　　DG2530 406
Ashkenazy　　　Decca SXL6603

Sonata in A, Op. 101
Gilels　　　　　DG2530 253
Solomon　　　　HMV XLP30116
Sonata in B flat, Op. 106
(*Hammerklavier*)
Solomon　　　　HMV XLP30116
Ashkenazy　　　Decca SXL6335
Eschenbach　　　DG2530 080
Brendel　　　　Philips 6500 139
Sonata in E, Op. 109
Myra Hess　　　HMV ALP1169
Brendel　　　Turnabout TV34111S
Sonata in A flat, Op. 110
Ashkenazy　　　Decca SXL6630
Solomon　　　　HMV ALP1900
Sonata in C minor, Op. 111
Brendel　　　　Philips 6500 138
Ashkenazy　　　Decca SXL6630
Solomon　　　　HMV ALP1160
Edwin Fischer　　HMV ALP1271
Diabelli Variations Op. 120
Schnabel　　　HMV HQM1197
Horszowski　　　Vox PL7730
Brendel　　　　TV34139S
Eroica Variations Op. 35
Curzon　　　　Decca SXL6523

BRAHMS, Johannes (1833–97)
Germany
Ballades, Op. 10
Katchen　　　　Decca SXL6160
Kempff　　　　　DG2530 321
Sonata No. 3 in F minor, Op. 5
Curzon　　　　Decca SXL6041
Variations and fugue on a theme of
Handel, Op. 24
Solomon　　　　HMV RLS701
Stephen Bishop　Philips SAL3758
Walter Klien　Turnabout TV34165S
Variations on a theme of Paganini,
Op. 35
Katchen (*with Handel Variations*)
　　　　　　SXL6218
Piano Pieces Op. 76
Piano Pieces Op. 116
Katchen　　　　Decca SXL6118
Piano Pieces Opp. 117, 118, 119
Katchen　　　　Decca SXL6105
　Op. 117: Bishop　Philips SAL3758
　Op. 118: Backhaus
　　　　　Decca Eclipse ECS691
　Op. 119: Bishop　Philips SAL3758

BUSONI, Ferruccio (1866–1924)
Italy
Elegies (*1907*): *Ballet Scenes No. 4,*
Op. 33
Martin Jones　　Argo ZRG741

192

CHOPIN, Frederic (1810–49)
Poland
Ballades
Ashkenazy   Decca SXL6143
Vasary   DG 2726 014
Kentner   Saga 5233
Etudes Opp. 10, 25
Pollini   DG2530 291
Ashkenazy   Saga 5293
Fantasia in F minor, Op. 49
Solomon   RLS701
Frankl   Turnabout TV34271S
Mazurkas cpte:
Rubinstein   RCA SB6702–4
Nocturnes cpte:
Rubinstein   RCA SB6731–2
Vasary   DG 136486–7
Scherzi
Vasary   DG 2726 029
Ashkenazy   Decca SXL6334
Rubinstein   RCA SB2095
Sonata No. 2 in B flat minor, Op. 35
Rachmaninov   AVM3 0294
Horowitz   RCA VH002
Rubinstein   RCA SB2151
Vasary   DG136451
Sonata No. 3 in B minor, Op. 58
Lipatti   HMV HQM1163
Rubinstein   RCA SB2151
Vasary   DG 136451
Waltzes
Lipatti   COL 33CX1032
Rubinstein   RCA SB6600
Vasary   DG2726 029

DEBUSSY, Claude (1862–1918)
France
Complete piano works
Monique Haas   Erato STU70605–10
Peter Frankl
                  Turnabout TV37023–8S
Children's Corner Suite
Arturo Benedetti-Michelangeli
                                     DG 2530 196
Images I & II
Arturo Benedetti-Michelangeli
                                     DG2530 196
Michel Beroff   HMV HQS1284
Preludes Bks. 1 and 2
Michel Beroff   HMV SLS803
Jean-Rodolphe Kars
                            Decca 3BB107–8
Bk. 2: Richter
                  Turnabout TV37027S
Suite bergamasque
Vasary   DG139458
Daniel Adni   HQS1262

FAURE, Gabriel (1845–1924)
Complete piano works
Jean Doyen   Erato STU70740–4

Theme and variations, Op. 73:
Barcorolles 1–11
Evelyne Crochet
                  Turnabout TV37040S
Nine Preludes Op. 103: 8 Pièces
brèves Op. 84:
Evelyne Crochet   TV37041–2S

GRIEG, Edvard (1843–1907)
Norway
Sonata in E minor, Op. 7
Alicia de Larrocha   Decca SXL6466
Lyric Pieces, Op. 43: Holberg Suite,
Op. 40: Ballade
Walter Klien   Turnabout 34365S

HAYDN, Franz Joseph (1732–1809)
Complete sonatas
in preparation
John McCabe   Decca IBB 100–2
Sonata No. 52 in E flat
Horowitz   RCA VH010
McCabe   HMV HQS1303
Sonatas 20 in C minor, 44 in G
minor, 46 in A flat
Rosen   CBS61112

JANACEK, Leos (1854–1928)
Moravia
In the Mist: On an overgrown Path:
Sonata
Firkusny   DG2707 055

LISZT, Franz (1811–1886) *Hungary*
Annees de pèlerinage (1st Year –
Switzerland)
Nos. 2, 4, 7: Kempff
                  Decca Eclipse ECS611
(2nd Year – Italy)
Nos. 1–7
Brendel   Philips 6500 420
Nos. 4–6, 10
Brendel   Turnabout TV34353S
Bagatelle without tonality
Brendel   Turnabout TV34232DS
Etudes d'exécution transcendente
1–12: Kentner
                  Turnabout TV34224S–5S
1–3, 5, 8, 10–11 Ashkenazy
                            Decca SXL6508
Harmonies poétiques et religieuses
(1834)
Kentner   Turnabout TV34310S
Harmonies poétiques et religieuses
(1852)
1, 3, 4, 7, 10: Brendel
                  Turnabout TV34246DS

Piano

Hungarian Rhapsodies
Roberto Szidon   DG2709044
Kentner   Turnabout TV34266–8DS
2, 3, 8, 13, 15, 17: Brendel
                        VCS10035
2, 6, 15: Horowitz   RCA VH006
Sonata in B minor
Curzon   Decca SXL6076
Vasary   DG2538 260
Brendel   Turnabout TV34232DS
Horowitz   RCA VH011
Pascal Roge   Decca SXL6485
Arrau   Philips 6500 043

MENDELSSOHN, Felix
(1809–47) *Germany*
Songs without words (cpte):
Variations sérieuses
Daniel Adni   HMV SLS862

MESSIAEN, Olivier (b. 1908)
France
Catalogue d'Oiseaux
Yvonne Loriod   Erato STU70595–8
Robert Sherlaw Johnson
                Argo 2BBA 1005–7
Vingt regards sur l'enfant Jesus
Michel Beroff   HMV SLS793
Ogdon   Argo 650–1

MOZART, Wolfgang Amadeus
(1756–91) *Austria*
Complete piano music
Walter Klien
            Turnabout TV37001–12S
Complete piano sonatas
Christoph Eschenbach DG2720 031
Ingrid Haebler   Philips 6727 001
Sonata in A minor, K310
Ashkenazy   Decca SXL6439
Lipatti   HQM 1210
Gilels   DG2530 061
Sonata in B flat, K570
Schnabel   HMV HQM1142
Sonata in D, K576
Ashkenazy   Decca SXL6439
Rondo in A minor, K511
Schnabel   HMV HQM1142
Ashkenazy   SXL6439

MUSSORGSKY, Modest
(1839–81) *Russia*
Pictures at an Exhibition
Ashkenazy   Decca SXL6328
Horowitz   RCA VH010
Richter   Odyssey Y 32223

NIELSEN, Carl (1865–1931)
Denmark
Complete piano music
Arne Skiøld Rasmussen
                Vox SVBX 5449

Three Pieces Op. 59: Chaconne:
Theme and Variations
Ogdon   RCA SB67

PROKOFIEV, Sergei (1891–1953)
Russia
Complete piano music
Gyorgy Sandor   Vox SVBX 5408–9
Sonata No. 6, Op. 82
Cliburn   RCA LSB4095
Sonata No. 7, Op. 83
Pollini   DG2530 225
Ashkenazy   SXL6346
Horowitz   RCA VH014
Sonata No. 8, Op. 84
Ashkenazy   Decca SXL6346

RACHMANINOV, Sergei
(1873–1943) *Russia**
Etudes Tableaux Op. 39
Variations on a theme of Corelli
Op. 42
Ashkenazy   Decca SXL6604
Sonata No. 2 in B flat, Op. 36
3 Etudes Tableaux: 6 Moments
Musicaux, Op. 16
Horowitz   CBS 72940

*In addition RCA have recently
announced the reissue in five albums
(three records each) of all Rachmaninov's records as a pianist and
composer–pianist. These are in-
dispensable to any student of the
piano.

RAVEL, Maurice (1875–1937)
France
Complete piano music
Robert Casadesus   CBS 77346
Gaspard de la nuit
Ashkenazy   Decca SXL6215
Browning   RCA LSB4096
Miroirs
Perlemuter   Vox STGBY622
Sonatine: Le Tombeau de Couperin
Browning   RCA LSB4096

SATIE, Erik (1866–1925) *France*
Gnossiennes: Gymnopedies: Avant-
dernières pensées: Heures séculaires
et instantanées:
Frank Glazer   Vox STGBY633

SCARLATTI, Domenico
(1685–1757) *Italy*
Sonatas
selection: Horowitz   CBS 72274
L21, 22, 118, 164, 187, 188, 203, 241,
349, 391, 424, 465

SCHOENBERG, Arnold
(1874–1951) *Austria*
Complete piano music
Gould   CBS MS–709

SCHUBERT, Franz (1797–1828)
Austria
Complete piano sonatas
Kempff   DG2720 024
Impromptus, D899, D935
Edwin Fischer
                World Record Club SH195
Kempff   DG139149
Moments Musicaux D780
Curzon   Decca SXL6523
Brendel   Philips 6500 418
Gilels   Angel 40082
Kempff   DG139372
Sonata No. 13 in A, D664
Solomon   HMV SXLP30053
Ashkenazy   Decca SXL6260
Sonata in A minor, D784
Ashkenazy   Decca SXL6260
Radu Lupu   Decca SXL6504
Brendel   Philips 6500 418
Sonata No. 15 in C, D840
Brendel   Philips 6500 416
Sonata No. 17 in D, D850
Curzon   Decca SXL6135
Sonata No. 18 in G, D894
Brendel   Philips 6500 416
Ashkenazy   Decca SXL6602
Sonata No. 19 in C minor, D958
Brendel   Philips 6500 415
Sonata No. 20 in A, D959
Eschenbach   DG2530 372
Brendel   Philips 6500 284
Sonata in B flat, D960
Curzon   Decca SXL6580
Brendel   Philips 6500 285
Wanderer Fantasia, D760
Richter   HMV ASD561
Brendel   Philips 6500 285
Jean Rodolphe Kars
                Decca SXL6502

SCHUMANN, Robert (1810–56)
Germany
Carnaval, Op. 9
Kempff   DG2530 185
Fantasia in C, Op. 17
Richter   HMV ASD450
Pollini   DG2530 379
Kempff   DG2530 185
Curzon   Decca Eclipse ECS568
Ashkenazy   Decca SXL6214
Humoreske, Op. 20
Kempff   DG2530410
Arrau   Philips SAL3690

Kinderscenen, Op. 15
Eschenbach   DG139183
Curzon   Decca Eclipse ECS568
Kreisleriana, Op. 16
Horowitz   CBS72841
Sonata No. 1 in F minor, Op. 11
Pollini   DG2530 379
Arrau   Philips SAL3663
Sonata No. 2 in G minor, Op. 22
Kempff   DG2530 348
Symphonic Studies, Op. 13
Ashkenazy   Decca SXL6214
Arrau   Philips 6500 130
Kempff   DG2530 317
Brendel   Vanguard VCS10020

SCRIABIN, Aleksander
(1872–1915) *Russia*
Sonatas – complete
Ogdon   HMV SLS814
Szidon (Nos. 1–4)   DG2707 058
(Nos. 5–10)   DG2707 053
Sonata No. 3 in F, Op. 23
Horowitz   RCA VH005
Sonata No. 5 in F, Op. 53
Richter   DG138849
Sonata No. 9, Op. 68 (The Black Mass)
Horowitz   CBS SET2002
Sonata No. 10, Op. 70
Horowitz   CBS 73072
Preludes, Op. 11
Ogdon   HMV HQS1296
Piece, Op. 45, No. 1; Etudes, Op. 8 (excerpts); Etudes, Op. 45 (excerpts); Vers la Flamme; Two Poems, Op. 69
Horowitz (w. Sonata No. 10)
                CBS 73072

SHOSTAKOVICH, Dmitri (1906–75)
Russia
Sonata No. 2, Op. 64
Gilels   RCA LSB4079

STRAVINSKY, Igor (1882–1971)
Russia
Three movements from Petrushka
Pollini   DG2530 225
Piano rag music; Serenade in A; Sonata; Four Studies
Noel Lee   Nonesuch H71212
Thomas Rajna   Saga 5335

SZYMANOWSKI, Karol
(1882–1937) *Poland*
Masques Op. 34; Metopes Op. 29; Etudes Op. 4; Fantasia Op. 14
Martin Jones   Argo ZRG713

Piano

TCHAIKOVSKY, Piotr
(1840–93) *Russia*
Complete piano music
Ponti   Turnabout TV37044–9S

TIPPETT, Michael (b. 1905)
England
Piano Sonatas 1–3
Paul Crossley   RCA In preparation
Piano Sonata No. 2 (1956)
Ogdon (*with Piano Concerto*)
                        HMV ASD621

Part Two

BARTÓK
Piano Concertos 1–3; Rhapsody,
Op. 1
Anda, Berlin Radio Symphony
Orchestra/Ferenc Fricsay
                        DG2726 005
Piano Concerto No. 1; Piano
Concerto No. 3
Barenboim, New Philharmonia
Orchestra/Boulez   HMV ASD2476
Piano Concerto No. 3
Katchen, LSO/Kertesz
                        Decca SXL6209

BEETHOVEN
Piano Concertos 1–5
Arrau, Concertgebouw Orchestra/
Haitink   Philips 6725 001
Barenboim, Philharmonia Orchestra/
Klemperer   HMV SLS941
Ashkenazy, Chicago SO/Solti
                        Decca SXLG6594–7
Piano Concerto No. 1 in C, Op. 15
Kempff, Berlin Philharmonic/
Leitner   DG138774
Katchen, LSO/Gamba   SDD227
Bishop, BBC Symphony Orchestra/
Colin Davis   Philips 6500 179
Piano Concerto No. 2 in B flat,
Op. 19
Kempff, Berlin Philharmonic/
Leitner   DG138775
Katchen, LSO/Gamba
                        Decca SDD227
Piano Concerto No. 3 in C minor,
Op. 37
Backhaus, Vienna Philharmonic/
Schmidt-Isserstedt
                        Decca SXL6190
Kempff, Berlin Philharmonic/
Leitner   DG138776
Rubinstein, Boston Symphony/
Leinsdorf   RCA SB6787
Piano Concerto No. 4 in G major,
Op. 58
Gilels, Philharmonia Orchestra/
Leopold Ludwig HMV SXLP30086
Badura-Skoda, Collegium Aureum
(forte-piano and authentic
instruments)   BASF BAC3002

Piano Concerto No. 5 in E flat,
Op. 73
Edwin Fischer, Philharmonia
Orchestra/Furtwängler
                        HMV HLM7027
Curzon, Vienna Philharmonic/
Knappertsbusch   Decca SPA334
Eschenbach, Boston Symphony/
Ozawa   DG2530 438
Kempff, Berlin Philharmonic/
Leitner   DG138777

BRAHMS
Piano Concerto No. 1 in D minor,
Op. 15
Curzon, LSO/Szell Decca SXL6023
Gilels, Berlin Philharmonic/Jochum
                        DG2530 258
Piano Concerto No. 2 in B flat, Op. 83
Richter, Chicago Symphony/
Leinsdorf   RCA VICS1563
Gilels, Berlin Philharmonic/Jochum
                        DG2530 259
Backhaus, Vienna Philharmonic/
Böhm   Decca SXL6322
Horowitz, NBC Symphony/
Toscanini   RCA AT103
Piano Concertos 1–2 (not available
separately)
Rubinstein, RCA Symphony/Krips
                        RCA DPS2015
Barenboim, New Philharmonia/
Barbirolli   HMV SLS874
Serkin, Philadelphia Orchestra/
Ormandy   CBS 77372
(with Violin and Double Concertos)

CHOPIN
Piano Concerto No. 1 in E minor,
Op. 11
Lipatti and orchestra (1948
broadcast)   HMV HQM1248
Pollini, Philharmonia/Kletzki
                        HMV SXLP30160
Vasary, Berlin Philharmonic/
Semkow   DG136453
Piano Concerto No. 2 in F minor,
Op. 21
Vasary, Berlin Philharmonic/Kulka
                        DG136452

Ashkenazy, LSO/Zinman
Decca SXL6174
*Piano Concertos 1–2; Andante
spianato and grande polonaise*
Rubinstein, New York Symphony
of the Air/Wallenstein
RCA DPS2034

GRIEG
Piano Concerto in A minor, Op. 16
Lipatti, Philharmonia/Galliera
HLM7046
Solomon, Philharmonia/Menges
HMV ASD272
Bishop, BBC Symphony/Colin Davis
Philips 6500 166
Curzon, LSO/Fjeldstad
Decca SXL2173

IRELAND
Piano Concerto
Parkin, LPO/Boult   Lyrita SRCS36

LISZT
*Piano Concerto No. 1 in E flat
Piano Concerto No. 2 in A major*
Brendel, LPO/Haitink
Philips 6500 374
Vasary, Bamberg Symphony/
Prohaska   DG2538 255
Janis, Moscow Radio Symphony/
Rozhdestvensky   Philips 6582 203
Richter, LSO/Kondrashin
Philips 6580 071

MENDELSSOHN
*Piano Concerto No. 1 in G minor
Piano Concerto No. 2 in D minor*
Katin, LSO/Collins Eclipse ECS627
Serkin, Philadelphia/Ormandy
CBS S72303

MOZART
*Piano Concerto No. 9 in E flat,
K271*
Ashkenazy, LSO/Schmidt-Isserstedt
Decca SXL6259
*Piano Concerto No. 11 in F, K413
Piano Concerto No. 16 in D, K451*
Barenboim, ECO   HMV ASD2999
*Piano Concerto No. 14 in E flat,
K449
Piano Concerto No. 15 in B flat,
K450*
Barenboim, ECO   HMV ASD2434
Piano Concerto No. 17 in G, K453
Casadesus, Cleveland Orchestra/
Szell (with K450)   CBS S61348

Brendel, Academy of St Martin-in-
the-Fields/Marriner (with K414)
Philips 6500 140
*Piano Concerto No. 20 in D minor,
K466*
Ashkenazy, LSO/Schmidt-Isserstedt
(with K238)   Decca SXL6353
Anda, Salzburg Mozarteum (with
K456)   DG138917
Brendel, St Martin-in-the-Fields/
Marriner (with K488)
Philips 6583 083
Piano Concerto No. 21 in C, K467
Casadesus, Cleveland Orchestra/
Szell (with K491)   CBS S61578
Anda, Salzburg Mozarteum (with
K453)   DG138783
*Piano Concerto No. 22 in E flat,
K482*
Barenboim, ECO (with Rondo,
K382)   HMV ASD2838
Piano Concerto No. 23 in A, K488
Kempff, Bamberg Symphony/
Leitner (with K491)   DG138645
Curzon, LSO/Kertesz (with K491)
SXL6354
*Piano Concerto No. 24 in C minor,
K491*
Kempff, Curzon (see above)
Anda, Mozarteum Salzburg
DG136196
Casadesus, Cleveland Orchestra/
Szell   CBS 61578
Piano Concerto No. 25 in C, K503
Barenboim, ECO (with K246)
HMV ASD3033
Piano Concerto No. 26 in D, K537
Haebler, LSO/Rowicki (with K453)
Philips 6580 043
Demus (forte-piano) Collegium
Aureum (with K246)
BASF BAC3003
Casadesus, Cleveland/Szell (with
K595)   CBS 61597
Piano Concerto No. 27 in B flat, K595
Gilels, Vienna Philharmonic/Böhn
(w. Double Concerto, K365)
DG2530 456
Demus (forte-piano) Collegium
aureum (with K414)
BASF BAC3066
Anda, Salzburg Mozarteum (with
K37)   DG139453

PROKOFIEV
Piano Concertos 1–5
Beroff, Leipzig Gewandhaus/Masur
HMV SLS882
Piano Concerto No. 3 in C, Op. 26
Prokofiev, LSO/Coppola
World Record Club SH209

Piano

Argerich, Berlin Philharmonic/
Abbado   DG139349
Katchen, LSO/Kertesz
                    Decca SXL6411

RACHMANINOV
*Piano Concertos 1–4: Paganini
Variations*
Ashkenazy, LSO/Previn
                    Decca SXLF6565-7
Rachmaninov, Philadelphia Orch/
Ormandy*   RCA AVM3 0296
*Piano Concerto No. 1 in F sharp
minor, Op. 1*
Janis, Moscow Philharmonic/
Kondrashin (with Prokofiev 3)
                    Philips 6582 008
Ashkenazy, LSO/Previn (with
Concerto No. 2)   Decca SXL6445
*Piano Concerto No. 2 in C minor,
Op. 18*
Richter, Warsaw Philharmonic/
Wislocki   DG138076
*Piano Concerto No. 3 in D minor,
Op. 30*
Horowitz, RCA Symphony/Reiner
                    RCA VH004
Ashkenazy, LSO/Previn
                    Decca SXL6555
Janis, LSO/Dorati   Decca SXL6057
*Piano Concerto No. 4 in G minor,
Op. 40*
Michelangeli, Philharmonia/Gracis
                    HMV SXLP30169
Ashkenazy, LSO/Previn/with
Paganini Variations
                    Decca SXL6556
*in No. 2, Stokowski

RAVEL
Piano Concerto in G major
Michelangeli, Philarmonia/Gracis
                    HMV SXLP30169
Marguerite Long, Symphony Orch/
Ravel   World Record Club SH209
Argerich, Berlin Philharmonic/
Abbado   DG139349
Piano Concerto for the left-hand
Katchen, LSO/Kertesz
                    Decca SXL6411
de Larrocha, LPO/Foster (with
Concerto in G)   Decca SXL6680
François, Paris Conservatoire/
Cluytens   CFP40071

SAINT-SAENS
Piano Concertos Nos. 2 and 4
Ciccolini, Paris Orchestra/Baudo
                    HMV CSD2750

SCHÖNBERG
Piano Concerto
Brendel, Bavarian Radio/Kubelik
                    DG2530 257

SCHUMANN
Piano Concerto in A minor, Op. 54
Lipatti, Philharmonia/Karajan
                    HMV HLM7046
Solomon, Philharmonia/Menges
                    HMV ASD272
Richter, Warsaw Phil/Rowicki
                DG138077 DG2538 025
Lupu, LSO/Previn   Decca SXL6624

SHOSTAKOVICH
*Concerto for piano, trumpet and
strings, Op. 35*
Ogdon, Academy of St. Martin-in-
the-Fields/Marriner   Argo ZRG674
Piano Concerto No. 2, Op. 101
Bernstein, New York Philharmonic
(with Ravel G major)   CBS 72170
Ogdon, RPO/Foster
                    HMV ASD2709

TCHAIKOVSKY*
Piano Concertos 1–3
Gilels, New Philharmonia/Maazel
                    HMV SLS865
Piano Concerto No. 1 in B flat, Op. 23
Richter, Vienna Philharmonic/
Karajan   DG138822
Horowitz, NBC Symphony/
Toscanini (rec 1941)   RCA AT113
Hass, Monte Carlo Opera Orch/
Inbal (with No. 3)   Philips 6500 196
Gilels, New Philharmonia/Maazel
(with No. 3)   HMV ASD3067
*Piano Concerto No. 2 in G minor,
Op. 44 (cpte)*
Kersenbaum, ORTF Orchestra
Martinon   HMV ASD2825
*in No. 2, Gilels uses the Silohi
version

TIPPETT
Piano Concerto
Ogdon, Philharmonia/Davis
                    HMV ASD621

Index

Piano

Piano

Piano